PROVISION
FOR THE MANY:
PERSPECTIVES
ON AMERICAN POVERTY

PROVISION FOR THE MANY: PERSPECTIVES ON AMERICAN POVERTY

W. A. Owings

University of Arkansas at Little Rock

The Dryden Press

Hinsdale, Illinois

PREFACE

With but one-seventeenth of the world's population, America commands nearly half of the world's annual income; uses nearly half of the world's telephones; watches nearly two out of every five of the world's television sets; could carry her entire population at one time in her private automobiles; maintains the most powerful balanced military force the world has ever seen; and affords an example of international beneficence unmatched in world history.

Yet there has been no time in our history when there has been such passionate outcry over the problems of poverty. Some authorities estimate that as many as one-third of us — nearly 70,000,000 Americans — live in poverty or deprivation. Yet America continues to face ballooning expenses for poor relief; in 1969 the number of welfare recipients in New York City, exceeded one million, and in a nation as a whole welfare expenditures exceed $100 billion annually.

How is it possible to reconcile those two sets of data?

However incongruous they may appear, it is obvious that the United States today is in the throes of a wave of welfare reform unmatched since the days of the second New Deal, if then. Since it appears that we are determining the welfare

practices that will be followed for at least the coming generation, it follows that we should review the entire question of
poverty and its relief so as best to determine on the basis of
human experience and reasoning the program that will most
effectively serve the interests of the whole community.

To the historian it seems odd that the current debate
over poverty is cast in the present, as if no one had ever dealt
with the problem before. The entire argument has been cast
in the two dimensions of the here and now; almost totally
lacking is the third dimension, *how it got this way*. This does
not mean that we need engage in empty antiquarian exercises.
A study of past experience is useful because we will find that
most of the present suggestions for dealing with poverty have
been tried before. As in all such studies, we can form some
ideas of the categories of solutions that offer themselves, what
has succeeded and to what extent, and what has failed. To be
sure, history will not afford us ready-made solutions, but it
does afford suggestive parallels. If we ignore the record, we
run the risk of passing over some very promising approaches,
and we also run the risk of making mistakes that have been
used before — "He who does not know history is condemned
to repeat it."

The lessons of history are useful only insofar as they are
applied to our unique condition. My second major purpose
therefore is to determine what the present state of affairs is,
and to examine the major schools of contemporary thought
with respect to the question of poverty. We can then assess the
advantages and disadvantages of each solution put forward,
and make the best possible projection of the probability of
success of each program. Such a systematic approach may be
almost offensive to many of the most vocal supporters of the
poor who, as we shall see, are acting more from the heart than
from the head. We may well be motivated from the heart,
whence indeed most motivations stem; but we must act from
the head, lest we create more problems than we solve.

My interest therefore is to define "poverty" and briefly
review the evolution of institutions for dealing with it in west-

ern civilization since ancient times: to describe the evolution of relief institutions in recent America; and to present a comparative analysis and critique of the principal contemporary schools of thought on reform of those institutions. I hope thereby to supply enough background to assist the generally well-informed reader in forming his own conclusions. An annotated bibliography is appended which the student might find useful as a bridge to more detailed studies.

Many persons have encouraged and assisted me in this work. The inspiration for it came from my observations at Resurrection City, Washington, D.C., in May and June, 1968, when for ten evenings I was the guest of the Highlander Center. The whole group, and particularly Myles F. Horton of the Highlander Center in Knoxville, Tennessee, were unfailingly courteous and helpful. My brief visits there provided me a deeply moving experience. My colleagues on the Faculty of the University of Arkansas in Little Rock who reviewed all or parts of the manuscript include T. Harri Baker (history), Agaton Pal (sociology), Robert E. Johnston (political science), the late Lloyd W. Bowie (economics), and W. E. Gran (physics). Edwin N. Barron, Jr., M.D., also read parts of it. Many students within the respective disciplines supplied penetrating criticism. The UALR Library was most prompt and efficient in supplying the materials I needed. Paul R. Baker of New York University supplied the final and invaluable critique. With so much competent and generous assistance available to me, any errors and deficiencies in the following book can only be my responsibility.

Little Rock, Arkansas
January, 1973

W. A. Owings

CONTENTS

PART 1

POVERTY
AND ITS REMEDIES
IN HISTORY

The Definition of Poverty

If we could only be sure that we all mean the same thing when we use the word "poverty," some of our areas of disagreement might disappear altogether and discussion of the remainder would be rendered much more fruitful. Unfortunately, views of the meaning of "poverty" are so variable that Theodore Caplow, who begins by defining poverty as "an insufficiency of the material necessities of life," immediately adds that "this is not a very exact definition because the necessities of one society may be luxuries in another and completely unknown in a

1

third. . . . The range of poverty may extend from starvation at one extreme to merely a family's failure to achieve the average level of living of a particular society at a particular time."[1] The conception of poverty thus extends to cover those who *feel* poor. This might include most of the great middle class of "affluent" citizens around the first of the month when the bills come due.

There are four principal categories of poverty:

1. Biological poverty constitutes deprivation of material necessities to a degree that threatens the health and life of the human organism. Medical care as well as food, shelter, and clothing come within the scope of this definition. This comes close to defining the poor in Darwinian terms, as those who cannot make a place for themselves in the ecological balance. Biological poverty may embrace entire populations most or all of the time; it may visit entire populations periodically; it may affect only a part of the population in a chronic form; or it may affect only individuals within the community.

It would seem to be relatively easy to define biological poverty, but actually there is room for considerable difference of opinion as to what constitutes it. For instance, we ordinarily think of a lack of nutrients as constituting the least common denominator of the definition of poverty. We also assume, however, that the "minimum" diet of the poor should include a daily portion of meat, but until recently meat was an unheard-of luxury in many parts of the world so far as the poor were concerned. An all-vegetable diet can supply all the nutrients the human body requires at a fraction of the cost of meat. If a community demanded that the poor be supported at the truly

[1] Theodore Caplow, "Poverty," *Encyclopedia Britannica* (1958), vol. 18, p. 392.

minimum level of nutrition, it would require that they subsist on a vegetable diet; but it is highly unlikely that our community would ever demand that the poor give up their meat. Thus there is a considerable cultural component even in establishing the "minimum" level of nutrition, and there is even more elasticity in the definition of the "minimum" requirements of clothing, shelter, and especially of medical care.

2. Relative poverty is the state of possessing fewer goods than another. One who is relatively poor may still be in comfortable circumstances, as an automobile-company executive with a six-figure income is poor in comparison with, say, the heirs of Henry Ford.

3. Subjective poverty, the emotional state that arises from the feeling of deprivation of goods in comparison with someone else, may result from relative poverty. Within limits, this subjective feeling is as important as the objective facts. It is a truism that wealth does not bring happiness, but it is also true that wealth can make one's unhappiness much more pleasant. Above the subsistence level, however, persons can be happy with a surprisingly modest level of consumption, and conversely a plethora of goods can still allow for considerable unhappiness. Unfortunately, there is no way of quantifying happiness; therefore there is no way really of getting at the heart of the problem of subjective poverty.

4. Spiritual poverty implies an overemphasis on the material aspects of life at the expense of higher human and spiritual values. It is easy to assume that the rich are by definition spiritually poor. Considerable support is lent to this assumption by the schizophrenic view of wealth taken by western civilization. Plato asserted that it was not possible to accumulate wealth by virtuous means; Christ took a dim view of wealth; the medieval church

considered "excessive" profit to be usury. This attitude has never prevented westerners from accumulating wealth, but it has made them feel guilty about being outstandingly successful at it. What is more to the point, it robs the relatively prosperous persons of some of their defenses against demands for redistribution of wealth.

Poverty in Primitive Societies

As in most social inquiries, it can be very useful to us to look to primitive societies for instances of the kinds of social adjustments that man can and will make. We must not press the examples too far, of course, since our society is a very large and complex one which may well call for correspondingly complex solutions to social problems. Nevertheless, the primitives can tell us much as to what to expect of man as man.

Unfortunately, the widely-differing conceptions of "property" and property rights make it difficult to assess the social meaning of inequalities in distribution of goods, and in many cases there is reason to doubt that subjective poverty exists at all. "In such primitive societies," says one observer, "the individual who, as an individual, is reduced to such straits that he must either depend on some agency set up for the purpose of preventing his giving way before the harsh dicta of the economic system, or starve, is rarely, if ever, encountered." [2]

There are two reasons for this. First is the intimate personal relationships afforded by small social groups. The family, the very basis of society, has the care of children

[2] Melville J. Herskovits, *Economic Anthropology: The Life of Primitive Peoples* (New York: W. W. Norton Company, 1965), p. 31.

as its most important function, and in human societies the aged nearly always have a claim upon the tribe for their support. Our society is marked by dissolution of family ties which extend beyond the range of the nuclear family; therefore the close familial relationships of the tribe are not available to us.

Second, and more pertinent for our purposes, is the operation of a human universal that all who are accepted as fully participating members of a society are entitled by right to a minimum level of subsistence. This fact is a consequence of the social contract, which lays reciprocal obligations and rights upon all who are admitted to full membership in the society.

Limitation of Liability

All societies must take account of the possibility that the problem of dependency might reach unacceptable proportions. Any society accordingly may wish to limit the proportion of non-contributing members who are entitled to support. The important qualifying phrase therefore is "fully participating members." All societies exclude or remove some persons from membership. Aliens and slaves, for example, are excluded. Furthermore, a society that feels itself to be pressing upon its ecological resources may use population controls. Historically, the most frequent control has been the denial to infants of admission to the society, using abortion or infanticide to dispose of the surplus. Once admitted, however, the society accepts responsibility for a minimum level of subsistence. That accounts for the fact that societies living closest to the margin of existence, and therefore suffering the greatest material poverty, show the least relative poverty. "In societies existing on the subsistence margin, rather, it is generally the rule that when there is not enough, all hunger alike; when there is plenty, all participate." [3]

Since societies limit their liability for dependency by excluding some categories of persons from full participation, it follows that societies might also limit their liability by disposing of categories of dependents they are no longer willing to support. The disposal of dependents, however, is rarer than one might expect. It is most likely to be accomplished by denying the means of subsistence to some of the society's members, and that is done only under circumstances of such extreme material deprivation that some members must be sacrificed in order that the rest may live. Certain of the Eskimos afford the best-known example.[4] We should keep in mind that all societies show a high degree of readiness to sacrifice the welfare of individuals for the real or fancied benefit of the whole. In contemporary America, for example, the operation of the draft system is one manifestation of that readiness; sliding scales of taxation are another. The possibility that large and modern social groups might decide to improve their general welfare by disposing of certain categories of dependents is certainly remote, but should not be discounted altogether.

The support of members of the society is arranged for by a remarkably wide diversity of devices for distribution of production, rendered possible by an equally wide diversity of definitions of "property" and property rights. The spectrum of social devices theoretically ranges from total individualism at one extreme to total communalism at the other. Neither extreme exists in reality. While many

[3] Herskovits.
[4] Margaret Mead (ed.), *Cooperation and Competition among Primitive Peoples* (New York: McGraw-Hill, 1937), pp. 72–76.

societies produce nearly all necessaries through communal activities, and all societies have at least some communal production, it is most frequently the case that the social assurance of necessaries extends to the means of support rather than the direct supply of the goods themselves. The most common example is the grant of use of land to a household as a matter of right. But even societies like ours, with a doctrinaire commitment to the rights of the individual to property, make the rights to surplus production contingent upon the provision of necessaries to all.

Nicholls' Principle

The clearest statement of that principle comes from an unexpected quarter. In speaking of the principles governing the reform of the Poor Law in Britain in 1834, Sir George Nicholls, one of the men most influential in the drafting and implementation of the reform, stated:

> It is accordingly an admitted maxim of social policy, that the first charge on land must be the maintenance of the people reared upon it. This is the principle of the English Poor Law. Society exists for the preservation of property, but subject to the condition that the abundance of the few shall only be enjoyed by first making provision for the many.[5]

The fact that the statement was made by Nicholls is particularly significant. He was not a scholar, but the retired captain of an East Indiaman who devoted his attention to service to the community. He was convinced of the necessity for guarding the rights to property and is identified

---

[5] Sir George Nicholls, A *History of the English Poor Law in Connection with the State of the Country and the Condition of the People*, 3 vols. (New York: G. P. Putnam's Sons, 1899), vol. 1, p. 2.

with the administration of the New Poor Law in nineteenth-century England and Ireland. He therefore represented the views of those who were most inclined to
refuse to the poor any right at all to community support,
and in his capacity as administrator of the Poor Law so
vigorously applied the devices for limiting poor relief
as to earn the severe condemnation of humanitarians. If
even he subjected the rights to property "to the condition
that the abundance of the few shall only be enjoyed by
first making provision for the many," no others can deny
the validity of that natural law. In his honor, therefore,
that principle will be referred to hereafter as "Nicholls'
Principle."

The Affluent Society

The "affluent society" is a catch-phrase that has been
popularized by the title of a book by John Kenneth Galbraith. He holds that we are living in a condition of affluence unique in human history and that the management of
our economic system must be quite different from that
adapted to an economy of scarcity. Galbraith does not,
however, define an "affluent society," nor does he bring
evidence to support the assumption that our condition is
unprecedented. A study of the primitive experience casts
light on both of those points. If one accepts the subjective
component in the definition of poverty, it necessarily
follows that if one doesn't *feel* poor, he *isn't*. To be sure,
in any society it is difficult to find persons who wouldn't
like to enjoy the use of more wealth. It is rather easy,
however, to find considerable numbers of primitive societies in which the majority feel themselves to be no worse
off than Americans living on a $10,000-per-year income.
The Bachiga of Africa, the Samoans, the Hottentot, and
the Maori afford examples. The Bathonga of Africa, for

instance, till, herd, and hunt. Game is plentiful. Women are needed to till the soil, and the availability of women is the only limit on production. The society is prosperous enough that the men can afford to be idle for nine months of the year, and so have considerable leisure to gossip and drink beer — a level of affluence that the middle-class American male is far from attaining.

We can therefore draw two conclusions. First, an "affluent society" is one whose participating members feel that it has achieved a reasonably comfortable ecological balance. Second, while by no means the rule, such societies are fairly common and can afford us some useful hints as to what to expect of our condition of affluence.

Sanctions in Primitive Societies

There is a common belief in our society that the whip of economic need is required to make persons produce. The examples of primitive societies suggest that this is indeed the most frequent sanction. Other sanctions, principally psychic ones, are also found. Pride is a major sanction; only recently has the expression of praise, "a good provider," lost its significance even to us. The obverse of pride is shame, which is freely used by many primitives, often to a degree as brutal as physical abuse. Scolding suffices to deal with minor deviations. Extreme deviation may call for banishment (nearly equivalent to death) and supernatural reprisal, but these are rarely needed for mere malingering. Those psychic sanctions, however, depend on the intimate personal relations characteristic of the tribe. Their applicability within our context is questionable. On the one hand, the sheer size of our society has led to alienation, permitting the socially-irresponsible person to escape psychic sanctions; on the other hand, our phenomenally rapid and comprehensive communications

systems promise to restore the possibility of developing
in-group feelings in a large community. Whether psychic
sanctions can again be made as effective as the whip of
necessity is an open question.

Poverty in the Ancient World

Slavery must be taken into account in any discussion
of poverty before the industrial revolution. Slaves usually
comprise only a small proportion of the population of a
primitive tribe, but the institution of slavery grew rapidly
with the introduction of the money economy about 2,500
years ago. In the Golden Age of Athens (ca. 460–430 B.C.)
slaves comprised nearly half of the inhabitants of Attica,
despite their marginal economic utility. They filled many
of the social roles that are today filled by the poor, but
the slaves did not have the claim to protection that citizens
did.

Slaves were supplied by two principal sources, the
first of which was war captives. The second source was
the community itself, with the decline of free citizens into
the conditions of bonded servitude. That social phenomenon was nearly universal in communities exposed for the
first time to a money economy. Credit is a powerful instrument for the improvement of an economy; but its use
requires a high degree of economic sophistication, and the
education of entire populations is a long and agonizing
process which usually leads through a period in which a
large part of the tillers of the land suffer from debt bondage. Until recent times the land was the principal economic resource, but it was useful only when tilled and
tillage required labor. A money-lender, therefore, was by
social consensus granted the right to compel persons to
remain upon their land and till it until his debts were

satisfied. With the high interest rates prevailing in the ancient world — usually more than 20 percent — and with the usual degree of human inefficiency and misfortune, let alone the chicanery which money-lending invites among naive peoples, entire communities could easily slide into unbreakable cycles of debt and the resulting debt bondage. Desperate peasants might find that their most practical recourse was to sell first their children, and then themselves, into slavery. As recently as 1649 the law code adopted in Russia had specifically to forbid the practice. Needless to say, the consideration of that provision was not the welfare of the bondsmen, but the desire not to permit the impoverished peasants to escape from the tax rolls.

Constitutional Reform

The Greeks of the classical age adopted constitutional reforms that alleviated the consequences of over-population and debt servitude. First was the codification of laws by Dracon. Those laws have become a byword for their severity, but the mere recording of the laws and provision of machinery for their execution afforded some protection to the weak from the whimsical abuse of the strong. More to the point were the constitutional reforms identified with Solon and Cleisthenes (ca. 594 B.C.). Their distinguishing feature was the provision for the participation of all citizens in legislative, executive, and judicial processes.

The state assumed the responsibility for making it financially possible for poor citizens to participate. All citizens were equally entitled to certain economic benefits, from which of course the poor profited most. Payments for many forms of public service were made, financed in part by revenues from the state silver mines. After the

Peloponnesian War (431–404 B.C.), a fee of three obols was granted for attendance at the Assembly, and attendance amounted at times to as many as 5,000 persons. Three obols was about the daily subsistence income for a family of four, but was less than the daily wage of a laborer. A juror received the same fee, and juries could number as many as 5001. The juryman's pay alone may have been the principal support of as many as 1,000 citizens. A similar fee was granted for attendance at a public festival. Therefore a poor citizen who faithfully attended all public functions need never starve; in a crude way those provisions amounted to a guaranteed annual income. Only citizens might participate in the benefits, however, and the rights to full citizenship were very restricted. On the eve of the Peloponnesian War the citizens of Attica totalled only about 45,000 out of a population of about 350,000.

An outright guaranteed income appeared only at Rhodes. The city of Rhodes was a prosperous trading port with its wealth based on the construction and operation of an unusually effective navy and well-managed diplomatic office. Peaceful relations between rich and poor were maintained by having the rich support the poor with maintenance grants of grain. The financing of the grants ultimately depended on the profits of an imperial system. Rhodes had subject possessions in other islands and on the Asiatic mainland which were not considered a part of the Rhodian political system; they were treated as colonies and paid tribute which was an important part of the income of the state.

The financing of public services in Athens, too, was linked in part with her imperial system. During the period when Athens dominated the Delian League (478–404 B.C.), the other members of the league contributed to a common fund for the maintenance of a fleet. Athens main-

tained the fleet as required, but there was a surplus in the
fund which the Athenians felt free to spend on public
works such as construction of the Acropolis, which gave
employment to the inhabitants of Athens. The Athenian
state was richest and her poor citizens most reliably supported when the Athenian empire flourished. Tribute from
subject territories abroad as well as subject classes at home
permitted the wide scope of Athenian participatory democracy. The citizens of Sparta also were supported by
the surplus revenues of the Spartan empire. We can conclude from these examples that assuming the obligation
for the support of the dependent classes of citizens can
encourage imperialism.

The Liturgies

The next most important device for alleviating conditions of poverty were the liturgies. Since the Greek city-
state resembled a private club of which the citizens were
members, it could be considered an association in which
the wealthier members were obliged to undertake the
more burdensome offices of state, including their financing. Thus a rich man might finance the production of a
drama, including the provision of tickets to citizens too
poor to buy their own, much as today the wealthy members of a congregation might contribute proportionately
more to the financing of their church. The reward to the
giver was the psychic gratification that comes from prestige; or conversely, punishment for stinginess was the
contempt in which the miser was held by the community.
The holders of liturgies were responsible for erecting public buildings, constructing ships of war, and in general
financing the expenditures of the public offices which
they held. The system was simply necessary in view of
the primitive nature of the ancient fiscal systems and

served its purpose well as long as the liturgies were voluntary. With the decline of the *polis* in the Hellenistic period, however, the prestige attached to the offices no longer repaid their cost; then the posts were filled by compulsion. That development was identified with the period during which Greece slid into chaos, misery, and obscurity.

The grain trade was the most important object of liturgies in both Greece and Rome. Shipping by sea was a very expensive and hazardous enterprise; shipment by land was even more so, and out of the question for bulk goods such as grain. Private enterprise left to its own devices found it profitable to ship only small-bulk, high-value cargoes of luxury goods. If the private merchant shipped grain at all, it was in order to speculate on the local famines that occurred frequently in a world in which communications were so precarious. Beginning in Greece, therefore, and later on a larger scale in Rome, the merchant was compelled to render a social service by devoting at least part of every cargo to grain; subsequently the grain trade became a major concern of the state. Consequently we can scarcely say that at any time during the classical period was the grain trade carried on in a free market such as prevailed for other commodities.

The *annona civica* was the name given to the grain liturgies in classical Rome. The development of the *annona civica* was closely identified with the impoverishment of the Roman peasantry as a consequence of the Punic Wars (264–146 B.C.), their drift to the cities as unemployed citizens, and the use of their vote by unscrupulous politicians. The situation impelled the attempt at constitutional reforms by Tiberius and Gaius Gracchus (133–123 B.C.). The latter introduced a complex program of reforms bearing on several problems with the intention of restoring the socio-political system of republican Rome in its pristine purity; it was therefore a "reactionary" program in the strict meaning of the word. The basis of the grain law was the principle that the state should assume the obligation for supplying grain. It was at first sold to the public at about half of the prevailing market price. That act attracted the mobile proletariat from all over Italy, so that the public treasury fell into serious difficulty. Gaius Gracchus proposed remedies which included the extension of citizenship to all Italians. This proposal turned against him his own proletarian supporters, who feared that with the dilution of their vote they would lose their leverage on the political system. As a result Gaius Gracchus lost first his popularity and then his life.

The supply of low-cost grain continued, however, giving way by 58 B.C. to its free supply. The relief rolls swelled despite every effort to control the illegal receipt of grain. When Caesar came to office (45 B.C.) he found 320,000 persons on the relief rolls; he reduced the welfare list to 150,000. Significantly, neither then nor later did any ruler of Rome, however powerful, dare tamper with the institution of free grain. Again, as in the case of Greece, the financing of the liturgies depended on the fruits of empire.

The liturgies in Rome extended far beyond the grain trade. Aspiring politicians often provided circuses for the amusement of the idle proletariat. Much of the routine administration of the empire came to be conducted through liturgies. By the second century A.D. they comprised nearly half of the administrative posts. At first the liturgies were accepted voluntarily, but as in Greece they eventually gave way to compulsory service, the state preferring to impose service on the rich rather than to pay salaries. Furthermore, the lower orders of trade-craftsmen and operatives were organized into *collegia* which had their places in the economic system; those in the all-important grain trade were particularly well-organized. The exploitation of the *collegia* was a part of the general system of totalitarian rule introduced by Septimus Severus (192–211 A.D.) and brought to full force by Diocletian (284–305 A.D.).

We have focused only on the aspects of the ancient system that have value to us in our study of the responses to poverty. There was much more to the system than these elements, and the whole is linked to the much-debated and never-settled question of the causes of the decline and fall of the Roman Empire. This is not the place to join in that debate. Suffice it for our purposes to say that Greek and Roman states alike assumed a high degree of control over the supply of grain and other foodstuffs to the community. In the case of Rome the particular manner in which the distribution was managed seems to have contributed to the pauperization of the Roman proletariat. That effect was at least not as evident in the case of classical Greece, and the Roman peasant had been impoverished, urbanized, and proletarianized long before he became pauperized. We are therefore not justified in inferring, as so many have done, that bread and circuses caused the decline and fall of Rome. Rather the administration of the *annona* and the other liturgies was conducted in such a way as to contribute to the trend toward totalitarianism. There is everything to support another common inference, however, that an idle and useless citizenry with only its votes to sell can be very dangerous to the stability of the state.

The Principles of Charity

The principles of charity that governed the support of dependents until our own time were fully developed by the later Roman period. In ancient Greece the distribution of relief was based on the rights of the citizen, no distinction being made at first between rich and poor. Consequently there are records of rich men appearing and claiming their share of public grants. In the chaos of the Hellenistic world in the first century B.C. the distinction between the poor citizen and the slave became blurred. We may speculate that it was in reaction thereto that the institution of slavery in both Greece and Rome first came under attack. By the first century A.D. there had developed the sentiment of *humanitas,* "a warm, human sympathy for the weak and helpless," [6] which was applied to the slave and poor alike.

Stoicism provided the philosophical foundation for the extension of aid to the poor. It embodied the idea of conformity to Nature and natural law as the rule of conduct. The worth and responsibility of the individual man were emphasized. It therefore entailed the idea of the worth and equality of all men everywhere. Social status and the material conditions of life were thought to be irrelevant to one's worth as man. Stoicism, with its emphasis on devotion to duty, was particularly appealing to Romans. They, and particularly Cicero and Seneca, carried it further by formulating the principles of justice and beneficence.

Justice regulates redress for injury, protects the property of the state and individual, and insists that the faith be kept. Roman conceptions of justice embodied moral and social imperatives, as when Cicero wrote "Justice com-

[6] A. R. Hands, *Charities and Social Aid in Greece and Rome* (Cornell University Press, 1969), p. 87.

mands us to have mercy on all men, to consult the interests of the whole human race, to give to everyone his due, and to injure no sacred, or public, or foreign rights, and to forbear touching what does not belong to us." [7]

With Cicero we come near to the argument for a moral right to public support. The instrument for such support was the exercise of beneficence, which was related to the doing of good outside of the sphere of justice. It was a way of alleviating social distress by taking direct, personal action: it enjoined upon the good man the obligation of generosity to the poor and unfortunate. The sanction required to make the injunction effective was internal; the reward to the giver arose from the sense of well-being that comes from generosity. It was recognized that the giving of oneself, in time and concern, was morally superior to the giving of money. Giving should be done in a way that would result in some permanent change for the better, rather than be a mere palliative of immediate distress; therefore the recipient of beneficence should be worthy of it. From that view stemmed Cicero's rules of charity: do not harm one whom you would benefit, do not exceed your means, and have regard to merit.

Christian charity embraced the principles of Judaism and Stoicism, and added features peculiar to itself. First, stemming from the idea of individual salvation, Christianity cultivated the idea of freedom and equality of individuals. Individuals, however unequal they may be on earth, are equal in the eyes of God, before Whom each must answer for himself on Judgment Day. Christianity did not, however, enjoin equality in goods or in status on

[7] Quoted in C. S. (Sir Charles) Loch, *Charity and Social Life: A Short Study of Religious and Social Thought in Relation to Charitable Methods and Institutions* (London: Macmillan, 1910), p. 115.

earth. Wealth was not to be accumulated beyond any reasonable limit; rather the rich were enjoined to love the poor and to give generously to their relief. The gifts to the poor were delivered to the church officials as God's custodians and by them redistributed as required by the needs of the poor. The sanctions enjoining generosity were ostensibly divine, and God's commandments were viewed with respect. In the small communities of the medieval and early modern period the priests wielded no mean social power as well, and the Puritan pastors particularly could be brutally frank in their sermons attacking the stingy.

The use of the church as intermediary had not been characteristic of the Greeks and Romans. The practice stemmed from the period when the church, still outside the pale of recognized institutions, had to care for its own members. There was little choice; if relief were to be afforded at all to members of an out-group, it had to be by themselves. The church thus lacked the support of state power to enforce redistribution of wealth to the advantage of the poor, but it also lacked responsibility for the welfare of the larger community. Its liability for charity was limited to the fully-participating members of its own community. As princes and their peoples were converted to Christianity the congregations expanded to include the whole community. In each state the church then was "established," that is, recognized as the branch of the state with responsibility for supervising the state of health, education, and welfare of the whole community. Through gifts, bequests, and grants by princes church institutions came to control great wealth which was ostensibly to be used for welfare. By the time of Gregory I (590–604) an elaborate administrative apparatus had evolved to manage the church's wealth and responsibilities. The decline of Europe into political anarchy in the middle ages permitted and required the church to continue as the principal agency for poor relief, but after its establishment it was never wholly free of state influence in discharging that function.

Millenarianism

The price of the growth of the church's power was an increasing elaboration and hardening of its administrative hierarchy. By the time of Charlemagne (771–814) the papacy was to all outward appearances a royal office, and the popes were claiming supremacy over secular princes. To many laymen it seemed that the church was forgetting its spiritual mission. From the very beginning of Christian history there has been an undercurrent of dissidence on the part of those to whom the formalism, luxury, and extravagance of the princes of the church are a scandal. Their unrest sparks the anticlericalism that appears even in the best-disciplined church communities. The unrest of those dissidents generally leads them to seek a return to the pristine purity of worship presumably found in primitive Christianity. Theologically, they easily drift over the border of heresy. By the twelfth century those tendencies had given rise to a number of heresies in which elements of gnosticism and Manichaeism were blended with Christianity. It is said of them that:

> The common characteristics of practically all the heretical factions were evangelical poverty, resistance to the secularization of the church and of Monasticism, the endeavour after a virtuous communal life, the rejection of the sacraments, dogmas, and authorities of official Christianity. . . . [there were many local variations, but on the whole] the conclusion may be drawn that this move-

ment whole-heartedly espoused the ideal of the primitive
Christian communities, rejected the principle of private
property and the social order based upon it, and aimed
at a communal life which would enable them to subdue
the material and to develop the virtues which their philosophy enjoined.[8]

The established church attempted unsuccessfully to
extinguish the heresies by persecution. In time the heretical tendencies were absorbed by the movements that were
precursors of the Reformation. There were several such
movements; a good example is afforded in England by the
Lollards, followers of John Wycliffe. Identified first with
religious egalitarianism, Lollardism afforded ideological
justification for economic and political egalitarianism as
well, as indicated by the couplet,

> When Adam delved and Eve span,
> Who then was the gentleman?

Certainly economic egalitarianism did not originate with
the popular heresies of the twelfth to fourteenth centuries;
the levelling sentiment is as old as man; but the heretical
movements crystallized the sentiments and afforded the
kind of ideological rationale that Marxism affords today
for similar social heresies.

The yearning for simplicity and purity in worship,
the repugnance felt for elaborate social institutions of
church and state, and the desire for a simple social order
based on economic and social egalitarianism, are widely
found to this day among simple folk. Among the peasantry
particularly such sentiments are often the basis of "primitive revolutions," especially of the anarchistic variety,

[8] Max Beer, *Social Struggles in the Middle Ages* (Boston:
Small Maynard and Company, 1924), pp. 136, 138.

referred to generically as millenarian movements. Millenarianism is not necessarily limited to peasant movements. In contemporary America much of the agitation for social reform is demanded, often in strident terms, as if the grounds for reform were universally known and accepted. Where no specific moral grounds for social reform are stated we can often discern millenarianism as the implicit and often unconscious basis. One striking contemporary example of millenarianism in action was the demonstration at Resurrection City in Washington, D. C., in the spring of 1968.

Poor Relief in Early Europe

Serfdom was the institutional framework within which the state attempted to deal with the problem of poverty in medieval Europe. Like slavery, it is a condition of bondage that makes comparison with modern poverty problems somewhat difficult. It represents an intermediate status between that of freeman and slave; the litmus test is bondage to the soil. It differs from slavery in that the serf is a fully-participating member of society, with rights as well as obligations. Humble men in the disordered conditions of the medieval period often actively sought the protection of the lords and out of fear of poverty gave themselves up to masters. The lords were obligated to afford protection, land, and civil administration. The serf had the reciprocal obligation of paying dues, which in an almost moneyless economy indirectly meant supplying the labor necessary to make land usable. Labor was thus a form of currency, and the lord therefore was entitled by right to the presence of the laborer on his soil. Hence the institution of serfdom.

In feudal theory the obligations of the lord to serf included a concern for his welfare, and on the whole the lords discharged that function as responsibly as the powerful usually do. Furthermore, the typical local organization was the village community, which performed many functions in common, particularly plowing and harvesting. Such communities were usually small, affording the same social sanctions as primitive communities. Between the mutual obligations of dependency and the communal aspects of village life, the poverty problem was most apt to take the form either of famine affecting the whole peasant group or of vagrancy on the part of masterless men who supported themselves by means of odd jobs or theft.

Vagrancy is the form in which the consequences of poverty are apt first to impress themselves upon the minds of the state authorities. Vagrants were not only numerous but socially dangerous. They were certain to be in need of relief at times, and in default of alms the vagrant inevitably drifted into petty crime. In an emergent economy lacking economic resources for the construction and maintenance of expensive penal institutions, lacking even the doubtful services of our rehabilitation agencies, and in an age generally more brutal than our own, there was little alternative to savage corporal and capital punishments. Therefore there was little latitude for distinguishing between various grades of crime, and if the vagrant drifted into petty crime, he had little to lose by passing on to major crime — he truly might as well be hanged for a sheep as a lamb. Police measures for the control of vagrancy were introduced by the state as early as 924, when King Athelstan decreed that every man who had no master should find one. In 1017 King Canute decreed that "every one be brought into a hundred," and made each householder responsible for all in his household, including strangers.

In the thirteenth and fourteenth centuries there were changes in the economy that led to the decline of serfdom and the subsequent rise of tenancy. The economic changes on the whole redounded to the benefit of the peasantry, increasing their independence of their feudal lords and leading to the decline of feudal secular and church Establishments. The merchant middle class and the journeyman-kulak class again became of significance. A manifestation of that phenomenon was the rash of popular revolts beginning in the thirteenth century which merged into the wars of the Reformation. Those developments paralleled the growing influence of the millenarian heresies.

The Establishment Reflex

The state Establishments attempted to discipline the lower classes by means of legislation intended to restore as much as possible of the conditions of serfdom. In England the pertinent act was the Statute of Labourers (1349), an act controlling wages and prices, which was also intended to deal with the problem of vagrants and beggars. The enactment of the statute followed close on the plague of 1348, and the preamble of the act complained that "many [workmen and servants], seeing the necessity of masters and great scarcity of servants, will not serve unless they receive excessive wages, and some rather willing to beg in idleness than by labour to get their living," and went on to direct that "valiant beggars . . . be compelled to labour for their necessary living." They were to be compelled to serve their customary masters at their customary wages, and on refusing to do so were to be jailed until they conformed to the law. Abandonment of service was to be punished by imprisonment; in later centuries this was expanded to enjoin "removal," or forcible return to the "place of settlement" (legal residence), not only of vagrants but of all who applied for relief. The Statute of Labourers was followed two years later by an act fixing in detail the wages to be paid for various kinds of labor, and in 1361 by laws imposing the punishment of branding with the letter "F" on the forehead, "in token of falsity," for those who violated the statute.[9] As late as 1530 a drastic law "concerning the punishment of beggars and vagabonds" was enacted. An able-bodied person having no master and no visible means of support was to be brought before authorities who might cause him to be "tied to the end of a cart naked, and be beaten with whips throughout the same town or other place, till his body be bloody by reason of such whipping;" and he was then to return to his birthplace or defined place of settlement to "put himself to labor like as a true man oweth to do." [10] It is no wonder that a nineteenth-century historian of the Poor Law was to observe that "this part of English history looks like the history of savages in America. Almost all severities have been inflicted, except scalping." [11]

Persons who were not able-bodied (the "impotent poor") traditionally were to be cared for by the church; but by the sixteenth century the church, caught up in the decay of medieval institutions, was no longer able to discharge its responsibilities to the poor. The act of 1530

[9] Nicholls, vol. 1, pp. 36–37, 42.
[10] Nicholls, vol. 1, p. 117.
[11] Nicholls, vol. 3, p. 13. Volume 3 was actually written by Thomas Mackay. Nicholls wrote only the first two volumes of the work attributed to him; the third volume is an addendum by Mackay relating his views of the operation of the New Poor Law in the nineteenth century.

provided that the impotent poor should be granted licenses
to beg within specified geographical limits. Licensed begging was an ancient institution and was socially acceptable
at the time because the church itself set the example of
mendicancy. Unlicensed begging was to be punished by
whipping. The determination of the authorities to prevent
it is evidenced by the provision that "scholars of the
Universities of Oxford and Cambridge that go about begging, not being authorized under the seal of the said universities, . . . shall be punished and ordered in manner
as is above rehearsed of strong beggars." [12] It's a pity to
spoil a good story, but it should be explained that students
in those days were in the minor orders of the clergy and
thus were part of a group that had social sanction for
mendicancy.

The Old Poor Law

The Theory of Secular Poor Relief

As so often happens with the evolution of social institutions, the system originating with the Statute of Labourers reached its fullest development just as it was beginning
to break down. The middle of the sixteenth century saw
the appearance of a more nearly modern approach to poor
relief. It was "modern" first in that it was secular, for the
church, also caught up in the decline of medieval institutions, had become far more a recipient than a donor of
charity. It was "modern" also in the systematic approach
to poor relief. The theory on which the new system was
based was put forward by a "brilliant Catholic humanist,"
Juan Luis Vives. He was familiar with the relief systems

[12] Nicholls, vol. 1, p. 118.

established in a number of municipalities on the Continent in the first quarter of the sixteenth century. In 1526 he published a long and well-received treatise on the subject in which he pointed out the danger of popular unrest under conditions of gross inequities in distribution of income. He urged the need of an accurate census of the poor and their division into classes of the needy, for each of which appropriate measures should be taken for moral as well as physical welfare, and he proposed reforms in relief administration in order to afford the funds needed for financing the relief agencies.[13] A number of cities including London adopted municipal relief plans that corresponded to that pattern. The form taken by English poverty legislation in particular owed much to that experience.

Queen Elizabeth's Poor Law, or the Old Poor Law, is the loose term denoting a configuration of traditional practices and acts of Parliament in effect by about 1600. The configuration included provisions for charity, poor relief, and settlement. The first two were the subject of the Charitable Uses Act and of the Poor Law, both enacted in final form in 1601. In accordance with medieval custom, it was assumed that relief of the distressed was the function of private charity granted in accordance with injunctions laid on the faithful by God, with the state theoretically playing a small role if any. Acts regulating public relief in the reigns of Henry VIII and Edward VI at first regulated only private charity; then such acts provided for voluntary contributions to a public welfare treasury within each parish; and later laws converted the

[13] Sidney and Beatrice Webb, *English Local Government: English Poor Law History: Part I. The Old Poor Law* (London: Longmans, Green and Co. Ltd., 1927) pp. 35–39.

voluntary contributions to compulsory ones, that is, a tax or "rate" levied on rent-payers. The acts of 1601 envisioned that provision of charity should primarily be a private function, with the state filling gaps only as required. Consequently as late as 1650, the year of largest Poor Law disbursements before the onset of the industrial revolution, only £4,306 5s were disbursed under the Poor Law, as against over £51,000 by private charity. In no year before 1660 was more than 7 percent of poor relief supplied by taxation in the areas whose records have been carefully studied.[14]

Beginning in about 1660, with the Restoration, economic practices foreshadowing the industrial revolution appeared and the system of private charity began to break down. By 1700 the Poor Law afforded the chief means of poor relief. Therefore the course of events was such as to transform a system of private beneficence through charity sanctioned by divine decree into a public welfare system through the Poor Law sanctioned by the police power of the state. The parallels with the evolution of liturgies in Greece and Rome are too obvious to be labored.

Settlement stemmed from legislation intended to compel laborers to remain in or return to their parish of legal residence and work at customary wages. As a by-product, that and subsequent acts determined also the parish responsible for the relief of each impoverished subject; and an applicant for relief might be forced to return thereto whether he willed it or not. Settlement provisions were codified only as late as 1661, but were substantially

[14] W. K. Jordan, *Philanthropy in England, 1480–1660: A Study of the Changing Pattern of English Social Aspirations* (New York: Russell Sage Foundation, 1959), pp. 131, 139.

in effect by the reign of Elizabeth. It is significant that the enactment of the Act of Settlement coincided with the period when the Poor Law assumed ascendancy over private charity in poor relief.

The types of relief afforded depended upon the needs of the recipients. Education (through the apprenticeship system) was expected to make poor children self-reliant. Parishes were expected to obtain raw materials for the unemployed to work up into marketable commodities; workhouses were established as the shops where such work might be done. The (parish) government thus became the employer of last resort. Since virtually all kinds of relief could be afforded at the discretion of the parish fathers, the Poor Law was by modern standards a very flexible welfare system. In general, it was customary to speak of the primary categories of in- and out-relief. Out-relief consisted of the rent-free or -subsidized use of cottages, grants of clothing and medical relief, and the like, with the recipient living meanwhile in the community. Out-relief might also include grants of money, including supplements to wages too low to provide a living. In-relief accommodated the ill, crippled, infant, and other categories of the destitute who could not care for themselves; those were housed in poor-houses and similar accommodations. In the American colonies it was a common practice to contract with citizens to maintain the impotent poor in their own homes.

The Old Poor Law in Action

How well did the law work? That is not as easy to answer as one might think due to the operation of a negative bias universal in polemical reformist literature. We take for granted that social systems should work well (by our own criteria). Our attention is aroused only when we are injured by their malfunctioning. Consequently the literature demanding reform invariably emphasizes the negative. Most of the literature we have on the Old Poor Law comes from two periods of reform. The first was in 1834, when reformers of classical-liberal, free-enterprise orientation were demanding a reduction or even elimination of publicly-supported social services. The second was from the first decades of this century, when socialist-oriented reformers were demanding extension of social services to the level ultimately of economic egalitarianism. Both groups were biased, and despite the fact that the biases operated in opposite directions, they did not cancel out. Neither group produced the evidence that would permit a dispassionate appraisal of the effectiveness of the Old Poor Law system.

The twentieth-century reformers were best exemplified by the members of the Fabian Society, which consisted largely of scholars of socialist orientation. They had the advantage of being able to rebut the arguments of the earlier classical-liberal reformers. They contributed vivid accounts of the fabled abuses of the Poor Law with its litany of homes and lives broken by the settlement acts, the prevalence of bastardy, the abuses of the apprentice system under which thousands of children were "apprenticed" to pauper trades under conditions that differed little from slavery, and perpetuation of conditions that dictated that few pauper infants would survive the first years of life.[15] Those conditions are rarely set into the context of the time. The seventeenth and eighteenth centuries were in many ways a brutal age by our standards, and

[15] See particularly Dorothy Marshall, *The English Poor in the Eighteenth Century: A Study in Social and Administrative History* (London: George Routledge & Sons, Ltd., 1926).

conditions might have been much worse without the Poor Law to blunt the worst effects of poverty. That it did at least that there seems little doubt. Furthermore, the worst conditions described were in the towns. For the most part the Poor Law seems to have been administered honestly enough in the countryside, and through most of the eighteenth century England was predominantly a rural land. We are justified in concluding that the Old Poor Law was as well-intended and effective a piece of social legislation as one might expect of the time and circumstances.

The Poor Law in the Eighteenth Century

The eighteenth-century experience with the Old Poor Law left three legacies to the nineteenth; workhouses, the principle of lesser eligibility, and unions of parishes.

Workhouses were long-established institutions. The Workhouse Test Act of 1722, however, was a permissive act under which a parish might not only establish a workhouse, but refuse relief to applicants who refused to enter it. The passage of the act was a response to the increase in the burden of poor relief. By 1700 the estimates of those receiving poor relief ranged from 100,000 to 300,000, and annual expenditures were believed to be £700,000. (Statistical data for any period before 1800 are very shaky.) Already rate-payers were expressing alarm and seeking ways to relieve themselves of tax burdens. In the seventeenth and eighteenth centuries there was a widespread belief that the costs of poor relief could be defrayed by pauper labor and that it might even return a profit to the community. Those hopes proved illusory. The workhouses never made a return on investment any more than modern prison labor does. The parallel goes further, for the workhouses were deliberately made so unattractive that persons would resort to them only in desperation.

The establishment of such unattractive institutions resulted from application of the principle of lesser eligibility. No taxpayer will willingly pay taxes to support an idle pauper in better economic condition than he enjoys himself. It follows that the standard of living of paupers is below that of the most impoverished taxpayer. When one keeps in mind the poor standard of living of the average Englishman at that time, it is obvious that in order to make paid labor attractive the workhouses had to be miserable establishments indeed. The lesser-eligibility principle was not stated so explicitly until the early part of the nineteenth century, but it governs the operation of poor relief systems at all times and places.

Unions of parishes were encouraged in order to meet the costs of building and maintaining workhouses. The erection of workhouses of any kind, let alone workhouses large enough to permit the categorization of the poor and their effective relief, required a capital investment larger than most single parishes could make. Therefore an act of Parliament brought by one Thomas Gilbert was passed in 1782 which permitted the union of two or more parishes. The unions then could afford to erect modern workhouses which would make it possible to administer poor relief in a humane and effective manner. A few unions were formed, and some reasonably satisfactory workhouses were operated by them. On the whole, however, the results of Gilbert's Act were unsatisfactory. It was significant as marking the beginning of a movement which in the end, through a massive reform of Queen Elizabeth's Poor Law, centralized Poor Law administration for all England.

The New Poor Law

The evolution of English social and political institutions was arrested during the wars of the French Revolution and Napoleonic period. The social stresses that accompany the transition of any emergent land to an industrial economy were compounded by those attendant on the massive conversion from wartime to peacetime operations. As the pioneer in industrialization, England had no precedents to guide her actions; she had to learn by experiment to adjust to rapid socio-economic change. Many thought she learned too slowly; there were numerous riots and rick-burnings by the poor. Massive increases in poor relief allayed the greatest distress, and many believed that the Poor Laws prevented revolutions such as those that broke out on the continent in 1820 and 1830. Relative placidity could only be had at a price, however, and by 1820 the taxpayers were complaining at the price.

The Wage Supplement

The most flagrant single financial abuse of the Old Poor Law was the wage supplement, a device which has recently been resurrected under the name of the Guaranteed Annual Income. At first a minor feature of out-relief, by the beginning of the nineteenth century the wage supplement assumed primary importance. It was an outgrowth of the wage-control practices of the late medieval period. Wages were limited to customary levels, which by the sixteenth and seventeenth centuries were often insufficient to support life; a man might have to work as much as two years to earn one year's living for his family. Since the wages were limited by the community, it followed that the community was responsible for making up the cost-of-living deficits. Then as now, "cost of living" was subject to wide difference of definition. Grants frequently were actually made on an *ad hoc* basis, in which the aggressiveness of the applicant figured prominently in determining the grant. For purposes of equity and efficient administration as well as economy, wage-supplement scales pegged to the price of bread were adopted by local jurisdictions. The one best-known today was developed by the justices of the county of Berkshire meeting at the Pelican Tavern in Speenhamland in 1795. In their table the cost of living was estimated to range from two shillings weekly for a spinster to 25 shillings for a family with seven children. The parish made up the difference between that scale and wages received. There were other scales, but that one has become so well-known that the system is often referred to as the "Speenhamland system."

The most provoking feature of the wage supplement arose from the fact that the poor rates were levied as a proportion of rent, principally on land. The rate-payers therefore were persons themselves in modest circumstances who were trying to accumulate investment capital. It was galling to them to see their profits bled off in taxes to support "the idleness and luxury of the poor" (charges laid against the poor at all times). Much more important was the fact that manufacturers had no need to pay a living wage if the community was compelled through wage supplements to make up deficits in the cost of living. In effect, the wage supplement developed into a device by which the community paid part of the wage costs of industry. That abuse was accentuated in localities where the manufacturers were the overseers of the poor and had the authority to fix the poor rates. The extreme example perpetuated in polemical literature by the enemies of the Old Poor Law was that of Colchester. There a living income was estimated to be ten pence per day; wages were but sixpence, the deficit being made up by the wage supplement. Consequently the poor rates amounted to 25 to 35 percent of the rents in that locality. Indeed, by the 1820s fears were being expressed that the poor rates would absorb rents altogether. Enemies of the Old Poor Law declared that just that had occurred in the parish of Cholesbury in Buckinghamshire, where the poor rate for 1832 was said to equal the rents; the parish fathers gave up, appealed for aid, and advised that the land simply be divided among the poor.[16] That's one way of impelling land reform.

The situation was really not nearly that desperate. It seems most likely that the poor rates increased from about £2,000,000 in 1800 to £8,000,000 in 1818, and after that fluctuated, declining below £7,000,000 in 1823, and not rising again until 1827.[17] As usual, however, political actions were determined by what men *believed* to be true. The prevailing belief among the rate-payers was that they were being ruined, and the fate of Cholesbury seemed to justify their fears. Inquiries made after enactment of the New Poor Law, and therefore too late to affect the arguments on it, revealed that to be a trumped-up case. The parish of Cholesbury consisted of only two farms totalling 110 acres.[18] Much more typical, and therefore much more to the point, were the marginally-successful farmers to

[16] Nicholls, vol. 3, pp. 65–66.

[17] J. R. Poynter, *Society and Pauperism: English Ideas on Poor Relief, 1795–1834* (London and Toronto: 1969), p. 287. He points out that the Speenhamland scale was little-known in its own generation, and acquired most of its notoriety retrospectively in connection with the arguments over Poor Law reform in the 1820s and 1830s.

[18] Brian Inglis, *Poverty and the Industrial Revolution* (London: Hodder and Stoughton, Ltd., 1971), p. 348.

whom a poor rate of ten shillings in the pound meant bankruptcy. They desperately feared a decline from the status
of independent farmer to that of dependent wage-earner.
They were numerous and therefore much more significant
politically than a stray parish or two in unusual circumstances. The resistance of those lower-middle-class taxpayers contributed substantially to the breakdown of the
Old Poor Law by the 1830s.

Poor Law Ideology

The ideology of the New Poor Law reformers comprised three principal factors: classical liberalism, Malthusianism, and scientific administration.

Classical liberalism was the doctrine emerging from
the eighteenth-century Enlightenment that emphasized
freedom, limited only by infringement on the rights of
others, as the organizing principle of society. This philosophy was taken up eagerly by the new industrialists who
saw an advantage in ridding themselves of restraints imposed by state regulation of the economy in the older
mercantilist system. Classical liberals asserted the rights
of property against the rights of status and tradition. They
contended that rights to property assured the individual's
right to enjoy the fruits of his own labor. The financially-
independent person also found it possible to maintain an
independent attitude toward authority.

The view of property as a liberating force is essential
to an understanding of the attitudes of Victorian England
toward poor relief. Many of us today view property rights
as antithetical to human rights; those who do so believe
that a man becomes the prisoner of his property. So he
may. He may as well become prisoner to any other idea —
and property, after all, is an idea like any other. To Victorian England the propertied man was a free man; to be

free was good for man; and therefore the truest charity to the dependent man was to enable, even to compel, him to be free. The argument has a Rousseauan cast.

Thomas Malthus with respect to poor relief argued that if population always pressed upon resources, it necessarily followed that grants of poor relief would increase the numbers of the poor. Poor relief, in fact, would tend to hinder the operation of the "preventive checks" such as delayed marriage which offered the only sure means of relief from overpopulation. Relief therefore was of no real benefit to the poor. The majority of mankind was condemned always to live on the margin of existence, and to increase their numbers through poor relief meant merely to condemn ever larger numbers to live at the same level of misery. The greatest kindness ultimately was to withdraw all relief and thereby to compel the poor to become self-reliant.

Scientific administration was a contribution of Jeremy Bentham, a tireless creator of elaborate systems. His basic philosophical principle was that of Utilitarianism — "the greatest good for the greatest number." For relief of the poor Bentham proposed a complete revision of the Poor Law. He had earlier developed a plan for a Penitentiary Panopticon for the confinement and rehabilitation of criminals; his Poor Law reform proposals owed much to the earlier plan. He would have established Panopticons for the poor, a network of large workhouses located ten and one-third miles apart (within walking distance of all people). The plan should begin with 250 houses, with 500 the optimum; each should hold about 2,000 of the poor. They were to be categorized into the old, invalid, blind, infants, and so on; and each should be afforded the support or corrective treatment suited to the category. The able-bodied poor should be set to work, and Bentham believed that their labor would defray the costs of the whole. His plan was never published, but it was circulated among his friends and young disciples, one of whom, Edwin Chadwick, was to become perhaps the most influential single person in the revision and implementation of the New Poor Law.

The principles of the New Poor Law did not conform to its ideology. A logical conclusion of the ideologies of classical liberalism and Malthusianism would have been abolition of poor relief altogether, and there were indeed some who advocated abolition. No one actually responsible for the conduct of affairs did so. Abolition would probably have provoked social revolution. The practical men of affairs recognized theory, paid it lip-service, and then took common-sense measures intended severely to limit the recipients of poor relief while still granting minimum support to the impotent poor.

The four principles governing administration of the New Poor Law were the abolition of out-relief to the able-bodied, who were thereby to be forced to become independent and therefore free; the workhouse test; the lesser-eligibility principle; and centralized Poor Law administration. Only the last was a novelty. Unions of parishes were to build workhouses large enough to achieve economy of scale and permit the systematic categorization of the poor. The enlarged workhouses were to be administered in accordance with directives of a board of Poor Law Commissioners with nation-wide authority.

The New Poor Law in action never functioned as its architects had envisioned. To begin with, the workhouses never were built in sizes and numbers sufficient to derive the advantages of scale. Usually the old poor houses continued in operation, more or less as directed by the Poor Law Commissioners. They could not categorize the applicants for relief as systematically as Benthamite theory required, and consequently the remedial efforts of the workhouses could not be effective. In theory they might have afforded superior housing, medical care, nutrition, and education. In practice, they did not do so; probably they could not have done so even had the effort been made; and most certainly they could not do so while the principle of lesser eligibility was applied, in view of the miserable conditions under which the poorest employed workers lived. In fact, public opinion would not permit a literal application of the lesser-eligibility principle in public establishments. Furthermore, the workhouses were still run much like prisons, the bitterest blow being the separation of husbands and wives to prevent the breeding of unwanted children. It is no wonder that where the workhouse test was strictly applied the relief rolls declined dramatically.

Differing interpretations can be placed on that fact. Some pointed with pride to the decline in the relief rolls, asserting that the poor went to work and were the better for it. Others asserted that horror of the workhouse drove the poor to vagrancy, to the harm of themselves and society. There is no statistical support for either view. What there is no doubt of was the hatred of the poor for the "bastilles."

The whole system was predicated on the assumption that the able-bodied must work; if no work was available, neither the workhouse test nor any other compulsion could be effective. Consequently in times of widespread unemployment the whole system broke down. When no other work was available, the ancient practice of made-work was substituted in the form of setting relief applicants to work on the roads or at breaking rock, thus substituting a labor test for the workhouse test. As usual, the made-work was of little benefit to the community and could do nothing to affect the existence of poverty at times of cyclical depression. The result was that the old system of out-relief remained in effect even for large numbers of the able-bodied.

Local vs. Centralized Administration

Critics of the Old Poor Law writing early in the twentieth century believed that many of its abuses stemmed from the use of local administration, which gave the widest latitude for neglect, brutality, inefficiency, and widely-differing standards of relief. There was among them an uncritical acceptance of the advantages of centralized administration, which they believed to have been demonstrated by the operation of the New Poor Law. Certainly centralization afforded advantages to a powerful reform movement seeking to influence the operation of the system, as the Fabians succeeded so well in doing. If we extend our horizons beyond the British experience, however, we soon discover social reformers working in other environments who demanded *de*centralization of administration. In fact, a frustrated reformer or revolutionary seeks a change in whatever administration exists. A historian has observed of the most prominent revolutionaries of the 19th century that

> in their political thinking Marx, Lassalle, and Proudhon each proposed to reverse the conditions of his own environment. Proudhon, living in centralized and authoritarian France, proposed extreme decentralization and democracy. Russians like Kropotkin and Bakunin, who came from a similar political environment, fell in easily with this anti-authoritarian element of Proudhon's thought. Lassalle, on the contrary, against the background of extreme decentralization of the German Con-

federation, was favorable to centralized state authority provided it be democratically controlled and exerted in the interests of the working class. And Marx, with English administrative decentralization and parlimentary government before his eyes, had a political ideal of centralized authority and dictatorship.[19]

Thus we can conclude that the views of social reformers as to centralization versus decentralization depend not so much on theoretical considerations as upon whether or not they have hope of manipulating to the advantage of their cause whatever system already exists.

The principles of the New Poor Law certainly had a profound effect upon the administration of poor relief, but as is often the case one is impressed also by the continuity of ancient practices across the trauma of formal change in institutions. At the turn of the twentieth century, some critics of the Poor Law argued that its defects were due to departure from the principles of 1834. It would be truer to say that the principles of 1834 had never been applied as theorists had envisioned and that the operation of the Poor Law system was always modified by conservatism, humanitarianism, common sense, and most importantly, the growing power of the working class.

The Working Class Helps Itself

At the beginning of the nineteenth century the working class and the poor were nearly identical. Their identity was reinforced by the fact that nearly every Englishman could expect to be touched by the Poor Law at some time in his life. Some working-class spokesmen developed the

[19] Robert C. Binkley, *Realism and Nationalism, 1852–1871* (New York: Harper & Brothers, 1935), p. 113.

theory that the poor were entitled by right to relief on grounds that the poor rates constituted their share of the rent on land. From that point of view the attempt through the New Poor Law to reduce welfare payments was construed as theft, and many of the poor workers believed that the reform was intended to keep them in servitude to the owners. This belief was perpetuated in socialist literature, of which Friedrich Engels' *The Condition of the Working Class in England* (1840) is the archetypal example. There is insufficient evidence to support an opinion as to whether the condition of the working class as a whole was worsened by the industrial revolution; that remains "one of the great unsettled questions of history." [20] Certainly many individuals, such as the hand-loom weavers, lost ground. Despairing of direct aid from the state, many of the working class turned to measures of self-help. Each of those measures is the subject of numerous special works; here we will merely mention and describe their distinctive contributions to the alleviation of poverty.

Political clout was the first effort of the working class, taking the form of the movement for a People's Charter. The immediate impetus for the Chartist movement was the electoral reform of 1832 which extended the franchise to forty-shilling freeholders. If to them, argued the working-class spokesmen, why not thirty? or twenty? or ten? or — why any property qualifications at all? Where does the right to franchise end? Nowhere. We now know that in that issue there is no golden mean; franchises are ex-

---

[20] Poynter, p. 27. Inglis does not come to grips with the question, although he clearly believes that the condition of the working class was much worsened. He supplies a fairly lengthy bibliography on the subject.

tended to cover all fully-participating members of the society. Proceeding in its usual deliberate fashion, the British community did not fully adopt the principle of universal manhood suffrage until as late as 1885. It is significant that the impetus toward state intervention on behalf of the lower orders of society is intimately associated with the extension of the franchise.

Unionism, next to political clout, was probably the single device most useful to the working man in lifting himself out of poverty. Briefly, the concentration of capital in the hands of owners was counterbalanced by the concentration of labor in the hands of unions. The consequences are too well-known to require elaboration.

The friendly societies evolved into institutions known in the United States as mutual insurance associations. As their name suggests, they were originally associations of congenial persons, often of the same occupation, assembling for convivial or religious purposes. Pooling of funds to spread the risk of medical expenses, burial costs, and the like, was at first a sideline; in time the insurance function predominated. Despite the fact that they were often covers for illegal combinations of labor, the social insurance function was so obviously useful that most European governments viewed them at first indulgently, and then with positive favor. In time they became so extensive that they were tied together into country-wide networks; they laid the foundations for the social insurance state established first in Germany under Bismarck. The United States was unusual in that it never developed an extensive network of friendly societies.

Cooperation has a long history. In the nineteenth century there were three major types of cooperatives. First were the consumers' cooperatives, for which the Rochdale Equitable Pioneers (1844) was the model. The association was able to make bulk purchases of goods and resell to its members at reduced rates, thereby eliminating part of the middle-man's profit. Part of the reason for their success was that retail trade was still primarily in the hands of small shopkeepers with their inevitable high mark-up in prices. The consumers' cooperatives therefore had a clear field for large-scale retailing. They have never flourished in the land of Sears, Roebuck. The cooperatives further reinforced their advantage by dealing at first only in the necessaries of life, for which there is a large and highly-predictable demand. Such operations can readily be routinized. In the twentieth century, with the growth of large-scale retailing even in Europe, the consumers' cooperatives have declined in relative importance (though not in absolute size).

Some nineteenth-century socialists, particularly among the Russians, placed great faith in production cooperatives, and there were numerous attempts to found them. Few succeeded, and none achieved the importance of the consumers' cooperatives. The difference seems to have lain in the function of enterprise. Industrial production in the nineteenth century was still anything but routinized, and few persons capable of managing an enterprise under the confusing conditions of industrial revolution would brook the frustrations of trying to manage a cooperative enterprise.

There were two major types of credit cooperatives, both of which originated in Germany in mid-century. Both were essentially what we call credit unions, the function of which was to supply cheap credit to peasants and small tradesmen. They were highly successful in performing that function; at the turn of the century there were over 30,000 in operation world-wide, and in some parts of Europe virtually all credit operations were in their hands.

The cooperatives served well in stretching the buying power of the working class. A condition of their success, however, was that they follow hard-headed business practices in extending credit; they had to resist the temptation to extend charity and thereby bankrupt themselves. The result was that the cooperatives did nothing to help the indigent; if anything, they contributed to the separation of the poor from the working class.

From Poor Law to Welfare State

As the barons had challenged the crown at Runnymede, as the squires and merchants had challenged the barons in the Revolution, as the industrialists had challenged the landlords in the first third of the century, so the working class challenged the industrialists in the latter third; industrial barons were confronted by labor barons. The result was predictable: the leaders of the working class were coopted to the ruling Establishment much as the leaders of industry had been coopted two generations before. By 1900, therefore, the working class had acquired much of the self-assurance and self-esteem of the upper middle classes — and like the *haute bourgeoisie*, it had left its origins behind. By the end of the century the working man had become literate, through collective action he had stretched his buying power and his power to bargain with proprietors, he had time and money for enlightenment and recreation, and he was protected against many of life's emergencies by the friendly societies. He had become part of a labor bourgeoisie. Beneath it was left the pool of the miserable poor. They were no worse off in absolute terms than they had been in 1815, but they were relatively more miserable as those able to deal with the capitalistic system worked their way into higher economic strata. By the

1880s the humanitarian reformers devoted their attention to the remaining poor. Their chosen remedies were to patch the system through private or public charity, or to change the system by adopting socialism.

The increasing affluence brought about by the industrial revolution had changed the terms of the arguments over welfare. Perhaps the most significant change was that at the beginning of the century the demands of the poor had been for bread, the minimum level of nutrition necessary for mere existence, while by the end of the century the question of bread had almost ceased to be a topic of debate. The arguments now concerned the supply of nutrients, living conditions, and medical care necessary for *optimal* functioning of the body rather than mere existence. Further, the idea insensibly was spreading that poverty, instead of being the normal state of the majority of mankind, was an aberration in social life that could readily be eliminated or alleviated. Some believed that the poverty problem could be solved by steeling the characters of the able-bodied so that they might become independent and that the impotent poor could be dealt with by private charity as their individual conditions required.

Scotland was taken as the model for enlightened charitable relief. Dr. Thomas Chalmers of Glasgow by 1823 had worked out a system whereby each applicant for charity was investigated to determine not only need but the kind of relief needed. Those "unfit" for charity were thus weeded out, and then the charity was afforded that best fitted the case. Charity might be a palliative, as in the case of the permanently invalid, but it properly should be of the sort that would enable the recipient to work his way out of his distressed circumstances and rejoin the ranks of the independent and self-reliant working class. The latter was the preferred goal of the charitable organizations; if the New Poor Law sought to compel self-reliance, the operation of charity was intended to make self-reliance a practical program.

In England, the rather haphazard operations of the individual charitable trusts were coordinated to some degree by the Charity Organization Society. For some forty years beginning in 1875 its director was C. S. (Sir Charles) Loch, who represented the interests of the charitable organizations in the investigations of 1905–1909 into the matter of Poor Law reform. He had little use for any sort of Poor Law, and in his *Charity and Social Life* presented as cogent a case as can be made for the use of charity instead of public relief to benefit the poor. No one reading his work can doubt his sincerity, but it is also an atavism completely out of accord with present views.

One of the lasting effects of nineteenth-century charity work was that by developing Chalmers' methods the private charities founded the profession of social work and contributed to the establishment of the techniques of the social investigations that flourish so in our day. Perhaps the most significant single exercise of the charitable spirit was demonstrated by Charles Booth, an eccentric shipping magnate, who manifested his eccentricity partly by his preference for the company of the residents of the London slums. He believed in the elimination of poverty, and at his own expense conducted the first of the massive statistical surveys of social problems. He introduced most of the techniques now in use, including the establishment of a "poverty line" and determination of the proportion of the population falling below it. He, like so many investigators since, concluded that at least one-third of London's population was impoverished. His estimate was confirmed for the city of York by Seebohm Rowntree.

Charity, however, on the whole proved to be a dead

end. Few really believed that voluntary charity would deal adequately with poor relief. Further, the investigations into the conditions of the recipients, especially when conducted by well-fed and well-dressed members of the middle class, were taken as degrading. Charities still exist, and their work is not unimportant; but with the decline of religion and the prevalance of the idea of the right of labor to a "rightful" share in production, the principal grounds for charity have been eaten away.

Contrary to the individualism implicit in charitable operations, however, and contributing to the acceptance of socialism, was the revival of state intervention in social affairs which had been dormant since mercantilist times. By 1890 massive urbanization with its demand for utilities, sanitation, and other public services, compelled social regulation of private behavior on a massive scale. The most portentious intervention was in the field of public education, necessitated by the demands of universal suffrage and industrialism. Paradoxically, the education of the working class demanded by industrialization increased its self-assurance and independence from the proprietors. The most important motivation for interventionism was the mobilization of the humanitarian spirit. If one assumes the psychic unity of mankind, there is no reason to believe that people at any particular time or place are inherently any more humane than any other, but the opportunity to exercise humanity depends on circumstances. By its collossal outpouring of wealth the industrial revolution made humanitarianism economically feasible; only an affluent society can afford to work toward more equal distribution of production. Biological poverty probably affected a much smaller proportion of the population in 1900 than 1800, but that merely sharpened the subjective poverty of the remaining poor and increased the embarrassment of the middle class that any distress should remain. From those factors stemmed the particular current of socialism that led to the adoption of the welfare-state principle in 1945.

Socialism

The definition of "socialism" is almost impossible to agree upon. Most treatments of socialism evade the problem of definition, assuming that the meaning is so commonly-known as to require none, or that opinions vary so much as to defy definition. Any serious reflection on the subject will make it apparent that a wide variety of social systems could be considered socialistic. For our immediate purposes we will adopt a vastly simplified conception of socialism. First, as to the spectrum of social responsibility that lies between complete individualism and complete collectivism, let us say that socialism comprises that body of socio-economic doctrines that leans toward the pole of collective social responsibility. Socialism particularly emphasizes the collective right to control the distribution of production, a doctrine for which John Stuart Mill afforded the theoretical justification. A corollary of this conception of socialism is denial of the significance of the function of the entrepreneur, or in some variants, at least the denial of the right of the entrepreneur to receive an "excessive" reward for performing his function. Most socialists also assert the necessity for collective ownership of at least the principal means of production. Those who distinguish between "socialism" and "welfare statism" make collective ownership the test.

Social control of distribution defines the least common denominator of socialism. It is such a broad definition that it includes all real societies. Thus publicly-owned systems of transportation, power, and education, can be

considered socialistic. Classical liberal opponents of socialism damage their own arguments because there has never
been a time when the most aggressive of entrepreneurs
did not demand social operation of many essential facilities. In fact, entrepreneurs invariably require that all essential facilities be operated at public expense if they cannot
be operated at a profit. In many cases, as in the operation
of the British coal mines and our contemporary urban
renewal programs, the business community demands that
the public accept responsibility for financing essential
facilities when their profit potential has been exhausted by
private enterprise.

It is equally true, of course, that there is no real-life
socialist economy that does not provide at least some latitude for private property and free enterprise. Thus in the
most communal of primitive communities there is acceptance of private property at least in personal possessions,
which may have considerable value. Among the major
contemporary socialist economies, even the Soviet economy at the height of the Stalin regime allowed the operation of small private enterprises, notably among the peasantry. Socialism need not preclude the existence of
entrepreneurs; it merely extends the right of eminent
domain to the productive function.

The social insurance state introduced important socialistic practices. It was the outgrowth of the consolida-
tion and extension of practices of friendly societies already
noted. It was fitting that it was introduced by the old
Junker, Bismarck, for in central Europe traditional status
patterns persisted despite the onset of the industrial revolution. Societies accustomed to a status heirarchy with an
upper class theoretically committed to *noblesse oblige*
regarded with indulgence paternalistic programs of care
for the welfare of the lower classes. More immediately to

the point was the domestic political situation. Bismarck's reaction to the rise of the labor movement under the direction of the Marxist-oriented social democrats was the hostility that he showed to the development of any powerful group not subject to his control, and in 1878 he had enacted the "Exceptional Laws" intended to control labor. But he was too clever a politician to rely upon the whip of repression alone. He attempted also to separate the laborers from the social democratic leaders by introducing social reforms. This is a particularly clear-cut example of the fact that sooner or later the need of the heads of state for political support, even of the poor, will give the poor leverage for bargaining to improve their conditions. By 1890 Germany had social insurance programs in effect for medical care, accidents, and old age and invalidity. Only unemployment remained outside the scope of the system. The social insurance system was considered socialistic even when it was limited to the voluntary cooperatives. In addition, almost from the first the state made contributions to the funds from tax resources, thus exercising a redistributive function by means of transfer payments. In practice, it has proved impossible for the state to refuse to extend redistributive practices.

The Fabians

The German idea of social insurance was taken up enthusiastically by the most influential socialists in Britain. Founded in 1883, the Fabian Society consisted of contemporary adherents of the utilitarianism of Bentham and J. S. Mill. They sought the greatest good for the greatest number in collectivism, involving state ownership of at least the primary means of production and the leveling of incomes to the point of economic egalitarianism. In their tactics they purportedly relied upon persuasion, and they had powerful persuasive tools at their command. In persons such as Sidney and Beatrice Webb and George Bernard Shaw they enjoyed the leadership of some of the most prominent intellectuals of the generation. Drawn in part from the *haute bourgeoisie* and the older landed Establishment, they enjoyed access to the highest circles of politics and society. Evolutionary in their orientation, they were content to use "Fabian" tactics of piecemeal penetration of established institutions and gradual conversion to the socialized and egalitarian society. Their chosen weapon was propaganda, and history has rarely seen as effective a propaganda organization.

But what would they do if propaganda failed? The propagandist rarely faces up to that question, but G. B. Shaw informed the "intelligent woman" that

> under socialism you would not be allowed to be poor. You would be forcibly fed, clothed, lodged, taught, and employed whether you liked it or not. If it were discovered that you had not character and industry enough to be worth all this trouble, you might possibly be executed in a kindly manner; but whilst you were permitted to live you would have to live well.[21]

If Shaw was prepared to deal so ruthlessly with the poor on whose behalf he spoke, what would he have done to members of the Establishment who frustrated his efforts? The quotation can of course be dismissed as one of Shaw's typically outrageous pronouncements, but it can equally be taken as a typical bit of Shavian realism. In either case, there is ample evidence from the record of elitist radical movements to demonstrate that the elitist when frustrated turns as readily to violence as does the rest of humanity.

[21] G. B. Shaw, *The Intelligent Woman's Guide to Socialism and Capitalism* (New York: Brentano's, 1928), p. 470.

The Reform Movement of 1905–1914

With the prevalence of the humanitarian spirit, the political clout of labor, and the guidance of the Fabians, the climate was ripe for another wave of reform like that of the 1830s. It would perhaps be better to say "counter-wave," for the principles of the new reform movement leaned toward the collectivist pole rather than the individualist. The old-style laissez-faire individualism still had its supporters, but not many, and they had much less effect than one might have imagined from the strength of tradition in British society in general. The individualists delayed the introduction of social insurance programs through the 1890s, arguing that the working man could and to a considerable extent already did provide for his own social insurance through the mutual-aid associations. They argued for the continued support of prudence and foresight on the part of the poor in managing their own affairs, on pain of impoverishment and miserable lives alleviated only by private charity for those who refused to care for their own futures. The humanitarians argued that the poor *could* not spare the income to provide their own disaster insurance; the individualists argued that they *would* not do so.

There was merit in both arguments. The poor, if not actually starving, were receiving well below the level of subsistence and medical care necessary to support human bodies capable of functioning at optimum efficiency. Significantly, the medical examiners of recruits at the time of the Boer War warned of the low physical state of the urban working class. J. A. Hobson in his seminal work on imperialism asserted that an industrialized and urbanized society would inevitably be handicapped in wars with states whose armies were manned by vigorous peasant soldiers. The desire to improve the quality of recruits available to the British army in an age of imperialism therefore played some part in rousing concern for the welfare of the poor among the authorities. To impose on the impoverished lower classes the added burden of safeguarding their own futures through compulsory social insurance therefore would only mean lengthening already-depressed lives at a slightly more inadequate level. The readiest alternative was social insurance financed by taxes.

There is also merit to the individualists' arguments that men *will* not care for their own futures. Old age particularly is a remote concern for the working man in the prime of life. Young persons caught up in the pressures of immediate needs to make their way in the world, subject to the more immediate demands imposed upon them by the care of their children, usually in the past committed also to giving their children a better start in life than they enjoyed themselves, easily drift into deferring the programs needed to assure their own futures. It can readily be argued both that they *should* take precautions against old age and that as beings subject to human fallibility there are many who *do* not do so.

Here humanity and common sense converge. Humanitarianism requires that individuals be protected against the worst consequences even of their own folly; thus state institutions afford relief and rehabilitation for victims of alcoholism and other drug addictions. That protection is doubly justifiable for the benefit of those who may, or do, suffer from the adverse effects of the free-market economy. The common-sense person more or less consciously admits that this attitude expresses a human universal. If the protection is to be granted, it is better that it be granted in accordance with an explicitly-stated rule, so that the community may know the kind and cost of its commitment. The argument therefore is really not whether to have social insurance, but in what form and how extensive. By the turn of the century the balance of opinion in England was shifting toward the provision of extensive social insurance by the state. It was within that framework of thought that social insurance legislation was enacted. In Britain the social insurance covered unemployment as well as old age and medical care.

The welfare state and the egalitarian state are the next most rigorous categories of socialism. The Fabians were always in doctrinaire commitment to their acceptance, and the welfare state was adopted in Britain in 1945. There are no egalitarian states as yet. The adoption of the welfare-state principle is the subject of much of the discussion of poverty in contemporary America; therefore we will defer its definition and discussion (see Part III).

Social Imperialism

The nineteenth-century European experience reinforces our appreciation of a phenomenon we have already observed: the influence of welfare programs on the promotion of imperialism. The expression "social imperialism" might today seem a contradiction in terms. In fact, it might even seem insulting to those accustomed to view imperialism through Lenin's eyes as a device of the bourgeoisie to extend their exploitation to a foreign proletariat and to use some of the profits to allay social unrest at home. The histories of poor relief in ancient Greece and Rome, however, showed that the relief was in part financed by the profits of empire, and therefore that the poor as well as the well-to-do had a stake in imperialism. We have noted also that the cooperative and labor movements were interested primarily in promoting and defending the interests of their own constituencies. To do so they were prepared to exploit other groups as necessary. After all, it was well-to-do humanitarians, not labor leaders, who inspired the discovery and remedy of the "poverty pockets." Most working-class activity was of course directed against the proprietors who controlled capital; but if the profits of imperialism benefited the working class, there was every reason why imperialism should be as popular with the masses as with the upper classes. The popularity of imperialism was reinforced by the spread of education and leisure. Universal literacy everywhere was accompanied by the growth of a jingoistic popular press.

Interest was reinforced by sentiment expressing the belief that the advanced European nations had the obligation as well as the right to extend the benefits of civilization to the inferior races. The idea that certain "races" (a word used almost synonomously with "nation" at that time) are superior is based on an organismic view of society. As a consequence, an Englishman or Frenchman or German of any class could take pride in belonging to a superior people with a distinctive historical mission. Such an outlook proved to be a major counterpoise to the concept of class conflict. The organismic view of society restores a corporate sense to the nation; it unites, where the class struggle divides. The sentiment of racial-national unity added still another motivation for the respective Establishments to concern themselves with the welfare of all their people, as a successful member of a family might feel impelled to find a comfortable position for an impoverished country cousin. An immediately practical matter, of course, was that the cultivation of national sentiments and the improvement of the human stock of the state was useful to the community as the period of conflict approached.

Interest and sentiment alike therefore account for the popularity of imperialism with the British working class. It required only a period of need and the development of a rational program showing some reasonable likelihood of profit to the masses to impel the adoption of imperialism. Those conditions were fulfilled during the 1890s. The Boer War and the tariff question brought the issue of imperialism to a head, and imperialism was advocated by some intellectuals now held in high esteem by social-welfare advocates. The membership of the Fabian Society was so divided over the issue that it never formally took a unified position; but a majority of the members were imperialists, and some of their opponents therefore resigned over the issue.

A generation later the world was to see what could happen when the racist aspect of the organismic view of society was driven to its psychotic extreme and made a basis of the policy of a great state. The organismic view of society is inherent in most socialisms, however, and biological racism is not essential to it. All other factors, and especially the factor of self-interest of the impoverished orders of society, are still in effect — in fact, they are human universals. It is important to keep in mind that social welfarism in recent as well as in past experience has lent support to imperialism. In the later nineteenth century imperialism was directed by the European states toward colonial lands. In the later twentieth century there is considerable anxiety in some quarters that social welfarism may impel imperialism on the part of emergent lands toward their former masters.

Conclusions

Our review of systems for dealing with poverty through the ages in a number of different socio-economic systems enables us to draw certain conclusions as to the kinds of response that we may expect to find in any society, including our own.

First, all societies adhere to Nicholls' Principle in affording a minimum level of material subsistence to all members admitted to full participation in the society (citizens), except in those very rare instances where the dire material want of a society requires the sacrifice of some so that the remainder may live. In order to meet that requirement, all societies limit their liability by imposing some check on the proportion of those admitted to full participation.

Citizens will not accept serious threats to life or health, and such threats provoke demands by the impoverished for constitutional and/or economic reforms that enjoin sufficient redistribution of wealth to fulfill Nicholls' Principle. Citizens may accept, or even seek, servitude as the device for assuring their security; but only in the direst circumstances, and they cast off their servitude as soon as possible.

Citizens do not demand equalization of material goods and will tolerate a considerable concentration of wealth in individual hands. We will not explore this avenue further, but Thorstein Veblen's *Theory of the Leisure Class* elaborates on the social utility of "maldistribution."

"Voluntary" charity can suffice for all of the redistribution that some societies require. There are always powerful social pressures enjoining "generosity," and there are also rewards to the giver, usually in the form of prestige. Charity has served well enough at other times and places to leave the possibility that it could also serve us as the principal means of poor relief. The western capitalistic and industrial society, however, has seen a transition from voluntary charity to compulsory redistribution under state auspices sanctioned by its police power. When conducted in a modern economic environment in accordance with systematic administrative procedures, the result is a Poor Law system. Industrial societies seeking institutional devices for relieving the poor tend to evolve through several stages to socialism: from individual responsibility to co-operative social institutions, to state-regulated and state-financed social insurance, to the state-operated welfare state, and finally to a socialist state, in which the state owns or controls the (socially-defined) "primary" means of production. The course of development would theoretically end with the acceptance of an egalitarian society, but none exist and none are in sight. In view of the manifest inequality in the natural abilities of individuals, it seems unlikely that there can ever be an egalitarian society. We might speculate that inequality might be expressed in other than material terms; we will consider that possibility later in the context of the contemporary American community.

Ideologically, such redistribution is rationalized by the concept of "social justice," which is intended to benefit the impotent or the "worthy" poor who can and will benefit by aid in such a way as to end their dependency. The concept of charity is also extended, although reluctantly and often without the sanction of philosophy, to "sturdy beggars," those who apparently could work but won't.

No community will accept an unlimited burden of poor relief; therefore all apply the "lesser eligibility" principle. Taxpayer resistance imposes a check on the proportion of gross national product devoted to poor relief. A democratic society is most sensitive to such taxpayer resistance. Authoritarian societies may be less sensitive, but in accordance with the law of politics that every government requires a minimum degree of consent for its operation, authoritarian societies too ultimately encounter an unacceptable degree of taxpayer resistance.

The greatest security arises from acquiring the strength to bargain or demand rather than beg. Self-help is a secure method of poor relief; the surest method is self-help through the exercise of political clout, the acquisition of which is facilitated by a democratic political order. Mobilizing the strength of organized numbers enables a large depressed majority to lift itself out of poverty. Paradoxically, improvement of the position of the remaining poor may be rendered more rather than less difficult, since *their* adjacent higher class now is a majority group which at best is not interested in their welfare, and which may even perceive the elevation of the poor as a threat to themselves.

The natural allies of the remaining poor, those at least one class removed, are most likely to be aristocrats and the *haute bourgeoisie*. Their spokesmen are most likely to be intellectuals drawn therefrom, who by virtue of their intellectualism always have ready access to the means of mass communication. The intellectuals particularly are convinced of their intellectual superiority to the *petit bourgeoisie*, and indeed to everyone else; they readily cultivate elitist attitudes. If they are unsuccessful in efforts to accomplish reform by manipulating the existing political system, they try first to change the system to something else. If again frustrated, the elitist intellectual may try to accomplish change by force. The result is *revolutionary elitism*, or the tendency of intellectuals to assume the moral obligation and right to alter social institutions as they see fit, if necessary by force. That is, they are prone to see themselves as philosopher kings. The behavior of the Russian *narodniki* after 1870 is the archetypal example.

The problems of poverty can be exported in the form of imperialism if it is believed that the profits of empire can benefit the poor. Imperialism can be especially attractive in a community in which the organismic view of society, as a unifying force, is being invoked as a counterpoise to the disruptive effects of class struggle. Intellectuals will rationalize a policy of imperialism if that policy seems expedient to them.

In the Christian community there is a permanent undercurrent of hostility toward formal social institutions and toward material and social inequality. In the Western Christian community that hostility is expressed in millenarianism. By its nature it is anarchic, and therefore can never appear as a coherent social force; but there is some content of millenarianism in all of us, so that appeals or demands made on millenarian grounds ring a sympathetic note and have more force than one might think from the numbers of millenarians involved. Millenarianism is also inherently romantic (emphasizing the emotional, or "natural," side of man's nature), so that it is impervious to rational arguments. The result is a fairly complete breakdown in communication between millenarian and Establishment spokesmen.

These conclusions on the evolution of poverty practices in Western civilization afford the framework within which the discussions of poverty reform measures are being conducted in the United States. Let us now turn to a consideration of America's particular problems in the twentieth century.

PART 2

POVERTY
AND ITS REMEDIES
IN AMERICA

America with its vast spaces, in
the eyes of Europeans virtually unoccupied, was regarded as
the land of opportunity for the aggressive and self-reliant, the refuge
of the persecuted, and a dumping-
ground for social misfits from the
fatherlands. The Puritan ethic, with
its emphasis upon the responsibility
of each individual to God, prevailed
to a higher degree even than in
Britain. In principle, the only obligation that any man would acknowledge was one he had freely
accepted by contract; having contracted, he could be held respon-

sible for the fulfillment of the contract to the last jot and
tittle. A man might own any property that he could purchase and enjoy it as he pleased. He was the freest man
the Western world has ever seen, and perhaps ever will
see again.

As long as there was an open frontier no able-bodied
man need starve. Since the dependent poor always are
cared for comparatively willingly, poverty was not felt to
be a grave problem. The absence of poverty was of course
a myth, although perhaps less a myth than most such.
Whether poverty was less prevalent then than now is not
possible to determine due to the shifting definition of
"poverty" and the lack of adequate statistical evidence
for the pre-Revolutionary period. As long as the society
was predominantly rural comparatively simple devices
could accommodate such poverty as existed. The problem
was accentuated in the United States as elsewhere with
the flourishing of the industrial revolution after the Civil
War. It was accompanied by all the familiar evils attendant upon the introduction of the factory system, with its
urbanization and proletarianization of the workers.
Roughly speaking, the evolution of social practices followed European models, although the American society
has been very reluctant to accept the full battery of welfare practices. Only as late as 1935 was social insurance
adopted on a national scale, and the 1970s await the open
acceptance of the welfare state. Our natural periodization
therefore is pre- and post-New Deal.

Before the New Deal

In the colonial period the attitudes toward poverty
were conditioned by the Puritan ethic, the lack of a status
society, and the value attached to labor. The Puritan

emphasis on individualism and the value of work as a good in itself cast the responsibility for one's well-being on the individual. Individualism was reinforced by the lack of a status society characteristic of the homelands; if men therefore were not bound to occupations by status, they also were relieved of status obligations to care for the welfare of the lower orders of society. There was therefore little of the paternalism so evident in Bismarckian Germany, and consequently there was a poor environment for the development of welfare institutions. The general tendency toward individualism and lack of community control/responsibility was reinforced by the high value attached to labor in a community in which few men had to work for wages. Most workmen were free craftsmen who could command favorable prices for their services. That encouraged the use of slaves and indentured servants; but slavery could be profitable only within the plantation system, and indentured servants eventually became free and also entered the ranks of the independent craftsmen.

Under those circumstances the need for relief was minimal, and formal social devices for granting it ranged from the casual almost to the non-existent. Rudimentary forms of Old Poor Law practices were followed, provisions being made for the apprenticing of poor youths and occasionally of poorhouses for the impotent poor. Throughout the nineteenth century, however, most of the inhabitants of poorhouses were indigent immigrants, a fact which lent incentive to the efforts of community leaders to "warn off" persons who might become charges upon the community. Perhaps the most common way of caring for the impotent poor in colonial days was to invite bids for their support, usually in the homes of the citizens. Various poor-relief services were then being contracted in Britain too. There the practice lent itself to some vicious abuses, but the system seems to have been used honestly enough in the colonies. The contracts did not provide merely for bare necessities. The overseers of the town of Danvers, Massachusetts, in 1767–1768 took into account the desires of the Widow Magery for some of the good things of life. She was a bibulous old soul, and "she drank altogether during the year 9 gallons, 1½ pints of rum and 1 quart and 3 gills of brandy, at a cost of £9, 13 shillings and 7 pence, old tenor. This thirsty widow had nothing to complain of even if she was short on other supplies."[1] No wonder America acquired the reputation of being a land without poor. There can be no more convincing evidence that the generous community supplies its paupers some luxuries.

The pre-industrial period of the nation was not marked by any substantial changes in poor-relief practices. Indeed, the importation of laissez-faire sentiments reinforced the attachment to individualism and the sanctity of contract. The prevailing belief was that as long as the frontier was open, the poor were so through their own fault; that poverty was due to idleness, extravagance, dissipation, and weakness of character in general. Relief continued to be a local responsibility discharged essentially in accordance with Old Poor Law practices. Consequently, most of the pertinent legislation was found at the state level, and usually provided for township or county relief systems. To that end, settlement legislation of Elizabethan severity providing for intrastate removal was the rule, and some grave individual abuses were perpetrated.

[1] Marcus W. Jernigan, *Laboring and Dependent Classes in Colonial America, 1607–1783: Studies of the Economic, Educational and Social Significance of Slaves, Servants, Apprentices, and Poor Folk* (Chicago: The University of Chicago Press, 1931), p. 204.

Some states also provided for exclusion and/or interstate removal; but that became a serious matter only at the time of the Great Depression, when a Supreme Court decision found exclusion to be unconstitutional. America therefore escaped the worst of those abuses. Otherwise, the only substantial change in poor relief practices in the nineteenth century was a gradual drift toward increased use of in-relief. In general, American poor relief reflected the same problems as the Old Poor Law in England. There were problems of settlement and inequalities in provisions for welfare among the states, with the more prosperous north-eastern and middle-western states the most generous. The programs were often administered by unpaid, uninformed citizens only remotely interested in welfare. The success of programs varied widely even in caring for the dependent poor, let alone salvaging those who might be returned to the community as contributing members.

Charitable practices too followed the English pattern, and as in England charitable activities originally were directed largely toward identifying the "worthy poor" and stiffening their characters so that they might become independent. The basic laws of the respective states that still govern charitable trusts were enacted then. The essence of the charitable trust is that it contribute to the public welfare and not be for profit. Otherwise there is little check on the trusts, and there has always been the possibility of serious abuses arising from lack of supervision. The functions performed by public and by private welfare agencies are practically the same; charity is not so much parallel with as indistinguishable from public welfare. The primary difference is that the charitable trust has no legal control over the person of the beneficiary; that condition imposes limitations in such matters as the disposition of dependent children. It has also been alleged that the charitable trust is the more handicapped by its relative rigidity (endowed for specific purposes); difficulty of financing; lack of public oversight; and lack of coordination of functions allowing some functions to be underendowed or overlooked altogether.[2] All of the latter, however, can also be true of publicly-financed welfare agencies.

The Advent of the Industrial Revolution

The generation following the Civil War began with the full flourishing of the industrial revolution in the United States; it ended with the closing of the frontier. Industrialization threw the strains on the social system that are commonly found in emergent lands. The period was marked by the growth of a labor movement and considerable social agitation. The closing of the frontier caused individualism to lose much of its attractiveness. There were therefore two powerful social vectors impelling a shift from the individualistic pole of social action toward the collectivist pole. By the turn of the century a marked change in the attitude toward the poor could be seen on the part of charity workers and social reformers. They were now inclined to attribute poverty to the operation of social forces rather than to individual deficiencies. The larger community, however, still held to the optimism reflected in the gay aphorism, "I've often been broke, but never poor." In a community in which a lack of money was held to be a temporary matter readily remedied by sufficient enterprise and hard work, there was no incentive for serious social changes. In retrospect, that optimism appears largely unjustified; there is now a con-

[2] Robert W. Kelso, *The Science of Public Welfare* (New York: Henry Holt and Company, 1928), pp. 96–98.

siderable body of literature describing the extent and hopelessness of poverty; but the reality did not materially affect the American resistance to state interventionism in matters of personal welfare. Oddly, and somewhat irrationally, the statement does not apply to education. To this day we are not accustomed to viewing public education as a welfare program, despite the ancient dependence of the Anglo-American community on education as the panacea for poverty.

The Impact of the Great Depression

The Great Depression was required to break the optimistic attitude. No one knows just how many men were out of work by the end of the Hoover administration, but the conventional estimate is that there were some thirteen million unemployed threatened by social degradation and stark hunger. It was a peculiarly brutal experience because the fall was from such a great height and because there was obviously no shortage of goods. In earlier ages there had at least been the justification of a physical shortage of grain to justify hunger; in depression America there was the prevailing likelihood of hunger, and some actual hunger, in a land in which a severe problem was the surplus of food. In fact, this was the most "luxurious" depression man had ever suffered. Even the poor on the whole were materially better-off than their great-grandfathers had been. But there was plenty of real deprivation, and fully as significant was the frustration of the millions of men able and eager to work for whom no work could be found.

This situation, it was widely believed, made a mockery of the suggestion of personal inadequacy as the cause of poverty. The popularity of demagogues and social reformers such as Huey Long and Upton Sinclair was evidence of the widespread disillusionment of the time. It seemed to many that man was the victim, not of nature, but of a defective economic system or the defective operation of it. If the system was made by man, should he not be able to control it? To the disillusioned it appeared that the businessmen who had assumed control of the system had bungled their jobs. Their panic at the collapse and their obvious inability to deal with it damaged faith in their competence even outside the ranks of social reformers, and investigations that revealed outright criminal activity damaged faith in their morality as well.

If confidence in the economic system was too great previously, disillusionment was perhaps too deep in the thirties. After all, the best and the worst that could be said of the businessmen was that they were fallible human beings. To them, however, had been attributed the full credit for the prosperity of the twenties, which was founded upon the philosophy of economic liberalism. They found themselves trapped in the dilemma of classical liberalism: if a man is totally free to achieve what he can, he is also totally responsible for the results. If his gains are due to his merits, his losses are due to his faults. Eager to accept credit for the prosperity of the twenties, business could not shun responsibility for the collapse of the thirties. No person who experienced the degradation of the depression could ever again have confidence in the competence of the business community to manage the economic system.

It is one of the ironies of history that Herbert Hoover first became known to the public during and after the first world war as administrator of massive programs of public relief. By the time he became president he was probably the individual in the world most skilled at managing such programs. He was also a successful entrepreneur deeply committed to classical liberalism. Since no one in the period 1929–1931 could know how deep the financial catastrophe was, it is not remarkable that under his guidance the primary efforts were directed toward restoring an economic system that had made Americans the most prosperous people in the world. In earlier panics the economy had been left alone and had recovered. Some of the most distinguished economic theorists of the day, notably J. S. Schumpeter, held that healthy recovery depended upon the economy recovering itself. Even today the esteemed Chicago economist Milton I. Friedman insists that the worst was past by 1933. He contends that the recovery would probably have been as rapid and healthier if nothing had been done to aid it and that the recovery measures of the Roosevelt administration were as harmful as helpful.

Perhaps. Now we can never know, of course, because the Roosevelt administration *had* to intervene in order to allay the distress. By 1933 the depression had prevailed for three years with no upturn in sight. America is the land of pragmatism. Whatever the Hoover administration was doing wasn't working, so something else had to be done — anything else, whether it showed promise or not. What was involved was another example of the prevalence of faith in common sense as against theory. Theorists might hold as they pleased that things would get better of themselves; hunger was an imminent threat to millions of households. The threat of hunger breeds the emotional state of anxiety, and human beings in the grip of anxiety must act to relieve the resulting tension — act effectively if possible, but in any event act, if only to be acting. Under such conditions theory is irrelevant. In retrospect we can only be surprised at the persistence of social tradition, which retained so much of the older economic system.

The New Deal

With the Roosevelt administration and its First Hundred Days came emergency relief measures entailing the expenditure of unprecedented billions of dollars. The officials responsible for the most important relief programs were the social worker Harry Hopkins and the Secretary of the Interior, Harold Ickes. Hopkins was a product of the Middle Border, the homeland of Populism, who liked to describe himself as "the son of a harness-maker from Sioux City." [3] His primary motivation was to get relief money into the hands of the impoverished citizenry as quickly as possible. For him, the immediate relief of distress was more important than the accomplishments of the make-work programs for which the funds were ostensibly spent, although in fact much useful work was accomplished by his Works Progress Administration. His ideas were antithetical to those of the notoriously irascible old Progressive. Ickes, "an indomitable defender of the national interest," [4] interpreted that interest as requiring that every dollar spent return full value to the community. His more crisis-minded colleagues could be driven frantic by his deliberation. Crisis psychology prevailed, and it was only as Roosevelt's first administration wore on that questions of principle began to arise.

Furthermore, principle was reinforced by political

[3] Arthur M. Schlesinger, Jr., *The Coming of the New Deal* (Boston: Houghton Mifflin Co., 1958), p. 265.

[4] Schlesinger, pp. 282–283.

expediency. The Roosevelt administration was threatened by the growing strength of social radicals. By 1934 the "Share Our Wealth" movement of Huey P. Long was rapidly gaining strength. He was supported by the anti-Semitic minister, Gerald L. K. Smith, and by the "radio priest," Father Coughlin. Long and Smith were products of the Deep South. That too was a homeland of Populism, a type of movement which would be considered agrarian socialism anywhere but in the United States. Rural America of the central and southern regions since the Civil War has had an affinity for such reform movements. Long therefore had a ready-made constituency to draw upon.

In California an old-age pension plan put forward by Dr. Francis I. Townsend appealed to a similar constituency. He "reached out to people raised in the traditions of rural Protestantism; assembled, they acted like a gathering of Methodist picnickers." [5] He appealed to a new force in politics, the old people. The birth rate was declining and demographers consulted by the government were inclined to believe that the population would reach its greatest size at a level between 146,000,000 (about 1970) and 190,000,000 (about 1980). The experts were inclined to favor the lower figure, and speculated that "it is even possible that the population will begin to decline after reaching approximately 146,000,000 in 1970." [6] The effect of such a population movement is that the population contains an increasingly larger proportion of the elderly,

[5] William E. Leuchtenburg, *Franklin D. Roosevelt and the Coming of the New Deal, 1932–1940* (New York: Harper and Row, 1963), p. 105.

[6] Warren S. Thompson and P. K. Whelpton, "The Population of the Nation," in the report of the President's Research Committee on Social Trends, *Recent Social Trends in the United States* (New York and London: McGraw-Hill, 1933), pp. 48–49, 57.

or demographically becomes "old." Politicians of the 1930s therefore believed that the vote of the elderly was becoming a force to be reckoned with.

Huey P. Long's movement threatened to draw three to four million votes from the Democratic party for a third-party ticket in 1936. The prospect was enough to chill the heart of any politician. The election of 1934, in which the socialist Upton Sinclair threatened to capture the governorship of California, further frightened the leaders of both major parties. As with Bismarck in the 1880s, the domestic political situation gave Roosevelt every reason to anticipate the radicals by introducing social reforms. The radicalism with which Roosevelt had to deal, however, was not the imported radicalism of Marxists and anarchists; it was the agrarian radicalism of the Middle Border and the Deep South, as American as apple pie. It followed that the particular reform measures introduced had a distinctively American cast. The most important single measure was the Social Security Act of 1935, which is still our basic national welfare program.

The Social Security Act

Unlike the earlier German and British social insurance legislation, the Social Security Act is an omnibus act with fifteen titles covering most fields of welfare. One title has been repealed, another absorbed into the Internal Revenue Code, and amendments have extended the social insurance feature; but the substance of the act is still in effect. The present debate over poverty in America involves the question as to whether there is a need for replacement or basic revision of that Act in accordance with a different philosophy.

The act was superimposed upon an extensive system

of existing welfare institutions and upon the massive system of emergency relief measures carried over from the first New Deal. A number of states had instituted programs of an experimental nature which they jealously guarded and wished to continue. There was also a strong doctrinaire commitment to the continuance of state control of the programs which arose partly from adherence to the federal system of government and partly from the belief that the federal system afforded desirable opportunities for experimentation on a comparatively small scale and for adaptation of legislation to local circumstances.

This latter point is often used today with dubious propriety — for instance, to rationalize racist practices, as in "the Southern way of life." It is a fact, however, that in a land three thousand miles across and lying in latitudes from the subtropical to the Arctic, still in rapid growth, and with regions reflecting many stages of economic development, there is justifiable reason for considerable variation in local social practices. For instance, the laws of water rights differ considerably between the well-watered East and the scantily-watered West. As American society becomes increasingly homogenized that consideration is diminishing in importance, but it must not be dismissed out of hand as irrelevant.

At the time the legislative proposal was developed there was considerable doubt that a national welfare program could be introduced at all under our Constitution. Frances Perkins, chairwoman of the Committee on Economic Security that drew up the legislation, almost despaired of finding a way around that roadblock. She found help from an authoritative source.

> I drew courage from a bit of advice I got accidentally from Supreme Court Justice [Harlan F.] Stone. I had said to him, in the course of a social occasion a few

months earlier, that I had great hope of developing a social insurance system for the country, but that I was deeply uncertain of the method since, as I said laughingly, "Your Court tells us what the Constitution permits." Stone had whispered, "The taxing power of the Federal Government, my dear; the taxing power is sufficient for everything you want and need." [7]

This anecdote is significant first as an example of flexibility in interpretation of the Constitution to fit changing circumstances; we shall return to this point in considering contemporary proposals for changes in the welfare programs. Second, it is significant that although payments by workers to the Social Security System are called "contributions," the Roosevelt administration not only considered them really to be taxes, but justified the whole program under the taxing power of the federal government.

Some critics of Social Security charge that the use of the word "contribution" to denote a tax was a bit of hypocrisy intended to enable the government, in installing its compulsory system, to capitalize on the good will that the commercial insurance companies had accumulated. Probably more important was Roosevelt's insistence on basing the whole program insofar as possible on accepted actuarial principles, thereby keeping it within the accepted framework of classical liberal doctrines. Roosevelt also had a practical political reason for insisting that the program be financed by its beneficiaries. By doing so he thought that those who paid into it would, under the principle of contract embodied in the doctrines of classical liberalism, have an inalienable right to collect at least

[7] Frances Perkins, *The Roosevelt I Knew* (New York: The Viking Press, 1946), p. 286.

some benefits. That was important to Roosevelt, who feared that a hostile congress would someday wreck his program. Frances Perkins and others argued against the inadequate levels of relief and financing by the payroll tax.

> "I guess you're right on the economics," Roosevelt explained to another complainant some years later, "but those taxes were never a problem of economics. They are politics all the way through. We put those payroll contributions there so as to give the contributors a legal, moral, and political right to collect their pensions and their unemployment benefits. With those taxes in there, no damn politician can ever scrap my social security program." [8]

Roosevelt himself was one of the most consummate politicians in the history of the American presidency. The whole transaction is an excellent example of the way in which politics affects the forms of economic programs, often to their detriment from a purely economic point of view. It is ironic that Roosevelt himself did not succeed in building into the program as ironclad a guarantee as he thought. We shall describe in another context a circumstance in which a "contributor" to Social Security has been dened benefits which a commercial insurance company would have had to pay.

The result of the conflicting political pressures was the development of a piece of compromise legislation which was superimposed on the mass of existing welfare practises. The Act did not completely satisfy anyone, but it was acceptable to enough interest groups to obtain the necessary support. Roosevelt and his supporters had no illusions. They accepted a very faulty program because

[8] Quoted in Schlesinger, pp. 308–309.

they could get it passed, and they expected that the program would in time be better adapted to reality as experience dictated.

Social Insurance in the United States: OASI

The functional categories of social welfare are: support for the aged, family and child support, health, unemployment, and "general assistance" or catchall programs of Poor Law origin. Due to continuance of substantial state and local responsibility, however, the Social Security Act provided for methods of administration that cut across all of those categories. Some are exclusively a federal responsibility; some are exclusively local; and in other programs the responsibility for funding and administration is shared in varying degree. Therefore there is no satisfactory way of relating social welfare functions to administration. It is most convenient and conventional to present the program from the federal point of view; that course will be followed here. The reader should bear in mind that the result is to diminish the apparent significance of the very substantial state and local programs.

It is best to consider the Old-age and Survivor's Insurance (OASI) program first, because it had on the whole the least opposition and best reflects our social insurance practices.[9] The program was designed to cover wage-earners, who are required to contribute to the program by means of compulsory deductions from their pay checks;

[9] The act was amended in 1956 to include a disability feature, and in 1964 to include the medical feature; the term "OASI" therefore is now replaced by "OASDHI" (Old Age, Survivors, Disability, and Health Insurance). "OASI" is still a familiar denotation, however, and since we are considering the old-age support programs separately, we will use it as a matter of convenience.

employers must match the contributions with an equal amount. The rate began in 1937 at one percent of the first $3,000 of earnings, in 1971 was fixed at 5.2 percent of the first $7,800 of earnings, and is scheduled by law to rise by stages to 5.9 percent of the first $9,000 of earnings in 1987. With the employer's matching contribution (which to him is simply a wage cost) the total OASI contribution in 1971 totaled 10.4 percent of earnings.

The funds collected are deposited in the Old Age and Survivor's Insurance Trust Fund, which invests the contributions in interest-bearing government securities. The total income meets current liabilities and also builds up a reserve, which in 1969 amounted to $30,082,000,000. The program therefore is ostensibly based on actuarial principles, as is a commercial endowment insurance program. There are some liabilities charged against the fund which are funded by appropriations from the general revenues, but those amounted to slightly less than 0.34 percent of the contributions for 1967.[10]

The maximum family payment that could be paid under the program in 1971 was a total of $434.40 per month to a widow with two children; the maximum individual payment was $250.70. The average payments are considerably lower. The highest average payment in 1966 amounted to $166.50 to families with retired husband, wife, and one dependent child, and $154.30 to surviving widows with one child. Individual retired male workers averaged $91.20 and female workers $70.70.[11]

The OASI program has aroused criticisms typical of those directed against all social welfare programs. The

[10] *Statistical Abstracts of the United States*, 1970, p. 289, Table 437.

[11] *Abstracts*, 1968, p. 284, Table 413.

critics fall roughly into three categories: those who argue that the program does not do enough, and does wrongly what it does do; those who argue that the program should not exist; and those who may or may not believe that the program should exist, but that it is wrongly financed.

The first category of critics are those strongly committed to social welfarism, at one extreme blending with those who argue for equalization of income and separation of income from work. They have three grounds for their criticisms. First, they charge that the program is not comprehensive. Persons not in "paid employment" are not covered, and appreciable categories even of those in "paid employment" are excluded. Presumably they are not concerned with the self-employed who do not choose to participate. The only employed persons not covered in 1966 were about 1,200,000 persons in agriculture and domestic service whose earnings fell below a minimum for coverage, plus an undetermined number of employees of nonprofit organizations. The proportion of the employed not covered amounts to something over 1.58 percent of those in "paid employment." No doubt it would be disproportionately expensive to administer the plan for the benefit of this small percentage, but there would seem to be no grounds for objection in principle to extending coverage to them, and certainly the proportion involved does not justify any very heated rhetoric.

The second ground for criticism by welfare advocates is that the poor whose incomes are below the statutory contributory limit are unable to make the full contributions to the plan, and therefore are not entitled to full benefits upon retirement. Their poverty in youth is perpetuated into old age. That, of course, is a fact; the implications of the fact must be considered within the framework of the larger question of the adequacy of the payments for anyone.

The third ground for criticism by welfarists is that at best the payments are insufficient to enable the aged to live in "comfort" and "dignity." That raises the philosophical question as to what price-tag can be attached to "dignity"; the social critics never attempt to define the term. We may avoid that question, however, by admitting that average payments substantially below $100 per person per month in 1966 did not afford much comfort; they could suffice only to prevent starvation. A partial response to that observation is that prudent persons provide for old age by other retirement provisions as well, such as paying off the mortgages on their homes while still earning wages, so that income does not necessarily correspond directly to consumption. The discrepancy between income and consumption is now being investigated more closely than before; results so far are inconclusive. The most substantial response to the charge of inadequacy, however, is that the Act was never intended to provide comfort. The original intention was to do precisely what is being done: to prevent the direst destitution, leaving it to the individual to make his own provisions for comfort and dignity as his personal circumstances and inclinations dictate. To do otherwise is to suggest that the individual be relieved of further responsibilities for his individual welfare, a suggestion that raises larger questions of principle.

The financing of OASI is attacked with equal virulence by supporters and opponents of compulsory old-age assistance. Its opponents charge that the supposed actuarial basis for the system is hypocritical; that, far from being self-liquidating, the system is really so grossly overcommitted as to be in precarious financial condition. Those who were already old when the Act was passed began drawing some benefits immediately. The benefits to the old since then have far exceeded levels that could be actuarially justified: that is, the benefits are financed by current payroll taxes. The fiscal device by which this is done is to deposit the funds in a Treasury account and to use them for the purchase of government bonds. Those in turn comprise the "trust fund" that is supposed to be the equivalent of the reserve that commercial insurance companies are required to maintain. In fact, the revenue from the sale of those bonds, as of all other government debt instruments, is used for the current expenses of the government. If the OASI were called upon to liquidate its reserves — if the government had to "buy back" the bonds held in the Social Security trust fund — it could do so only with funds derived from current tax revenues. The reserve therefore is no stronger than the government's current tax situation. The processing of the funds through a Treasury account is believed by opponents of compulsory old-age assistance to be nothing but a bit of fiscal legerdemain. At present the payroll tax can be borne rather readily, for the children born during the great post-war baby boom are now entering the work force. The members of the present parental generation can expect to have their old age secured by the "contributions" of their children. Those children, however — those now in their twenties — are accumulating a huge liability against the fund, and the birth rate was sharply declining in the later 1960s. Opponents of OASI therefore issue dark warnings of a total bankruptcy of the system as the baby-boom generation ages. Indeed, it has been charged that the Social Security system already is actuarially bankrupt.

Advocates of extended welfare view the situation with equanimity, because they never believed in payroll-tax financing anyway. Aside from the low level of relief, their objection is that the payroll tax is a "regressive" tax, i.e., one levied against the first increment of income, which therefore accentuates rather than alleviates income mal-distribution. Welfarists generally also believe in income equalization and would much prefer to see the Social Security system financed by general revenues derived from a graduated income tax. Obviously, the government cannot refuse to honor the claims against OASI as they come due and will have to resort to financing from the general revenues when necessary. A "bankruptcy" of OASI would mean nothing more than elimination of a pseudo-actuarial system, a thing which most advocates of extended welfare seek anyway on doctrinaire grounds.

Eliminating the actuarial features implies abandonment of the principle of social insurance, the argument being that the aged are entitled by right to a share, in the view of some an equal share, in the distribution of national income. They assert that the aged during their productive years invested their time and efforts in the economy to the benefit of the whole community; that in effect they made an investment in the total economy; and like any shareholders are entitled to the profits on their investment. That view received judicial sanction in the following words of a Supreme Court decision:

> But each worker's benefits, though flowing from the contributions he made to the national economy while actively employed, are not dependent on the degree to which he was called upon to support the system by taxation. . . . The "right" to Social Security benefits rests on the legislative judgment that those who in their productive years were functioning members of the economy may justly call upon that economy, in their later years, for

protection from "the rigors of the poor house as well as from the haunting fear that such a lot awaits them when journey's end is near." [12]

According to that view, the share of the old should not be limited by an actuarial return fixed at an earlier time when the dollar was worth more and before they could cash in on the prosperity to which they had contributed. This in turn requires the denial either that some individuals contribute more to the economy than others, or that superior contributions deserve superior awards. This translates the argument to the larger philosophical debate between the socialists and the economic libertarians.

There remain those committed to the principles of economic libertarianism who argue against having any kind of compulsory pension programs for the aged. The leading spokesman for that school is Milton I. Friedman of the University of Chicago, today the best-regarded advocate of the most complete possible economic freedom coupled with the most complete possible economic responsibility. The argument is a familiar one: it is good for humans to be free, and a man cannot be free if he is economically dependent. Compulsory contributory plans bind his liberty; therefore they are unacceptable. They are particularly unacceptable when they are designed to guard a person's welfare, against his will, against such a predictable contingency as old age. The free man may reasonably be charged with guarding his own future, and if he fails to do so, he may reasonably be expected to suffer the natural consequences of his own poor judgment. He has no moral right to expect the community to protect him from the consequences of his own folly.

[12] *Flemming v. Nestor,* 363 U. S. 610; the internal quotation is from *Helvering v. Davis,* 301 U. S. 641.

However impeccable the philosophical argument may be, it encounters the very practical objection that human beings are human. It is possible for an intelligent person to acknowledge that he will one day become old, yet make no provision for the day. Old age is a remote concern for the young, and it is particularly difficult to induce them to reserve retirement funds at ages when they are hard-pressed to meet the more immediate problems of making a career and raising a family. The best example of the neglect of old-age provisions comes from the university community. Many university faculties in the United States have their retirement benefits provided through a contributory program administered by the Teacher's Insurance and Annuity Association (TIAA). TIAA provides for either voluntary or compulsory participation by the faculty members at the discretion of the institutions. TIAA advises that the institutions require compulsory participation, however. Experience has shown that many faculty members will not participate voluntarily, but at retirement nevertheless lay a claim against the institution on grounds of their years of faithful service. The institution can rarely refuse such claims, so prudent administrations protect the interest of the professors by requiring participation. Now, of all social groups whose business it is to exercise foresight, academia stands first. If professors will not take prudent measures to protect themselves against such a predictable contingency as old age, who among them would admit that laborers would be any more prudent? To expect society to make up for their folly is not moral (from the classical liberal point of view), but it is very human; and it is to be expected that when such demands are sufficiently widespread they will be met by politicians. It therefore appears that Friedman's arguments against compulsory old-age programs do not meet the test of common sense. In fact, Friedman himself does not press his argument to its logical conclusion, since the form of Guaranteed Annual Income that he advocates would provide for noncontributory assistance. It appears that some kind of old-age assistance is inevitable, if not because it is just, then because it is expedient. The same may be said of many other welfare programs.

Federal Responsibility: Veterans' Programs

Veterans' benefits are contingent upon having served in the armed forces and ostensibly are intended to repair the damage suffered by the individual in health or loss of time in rendering that public service. Thus there is an important contractual aspect to veteran's benefits. Persons who are exposed to unusual discomfort and risks in the public interest are legitimately entitled to some special recognition of their services. Veterans' benefits are reported statistically as a part of the nation's welfare expenditures, however, and the political pressures brought to bear by veterans' groups have resulted in practices such as medical care for indigent veterans that are much the same as other welfare services. In 1967 the expenditures were just over $7 billion, about 7 percent of the total national governmental welfare expenditures. Of that, just over 4 billion was spent for pensions and about 1.25 billion for medical care. Insofar as low-income persons benefited from the programs they presumably made a substantial, though undetermined, contribution toward easing the problems of poverty. Since the military services normally require that recruits be taken from the upper half, or at worst the upper two-thirds, of the population as defined by physical condition and ability to pass mental examinations, the operation of the veterans' programs probably fails to reach the very hard-core poor.

The State-Federal Mix

All social security programs other than OASI and the VA share responsibility between the state and federal governments. They are often administered locally under state laws drawn to meet minimum federal specifications. Financing of the programs also involves a mix of funds from both sources. The federal funds are usually disbursed in the form of grants to the states contingent upon the states appropriating a matching fund. As a result, there can be considerable unevenness in the benefits and coverage of the programs among states. The proportion granted by the federal government varies with the program, but it is always large and in some programs amounts to nearly all of the financing.

Medical Care

The general assistance programs of Poor Law origin and the traditional practices of charitable aid by private institutions and practitioners have made available to the poor massive amounts of medical aid at the state and local levels. Nevertheless social reformers since the turn of the century have been increasingly insistent that the federal government assume a major responsibility in that area. The Perkins committee considered the adoption of federal medical aid to the indigent when the Social Security act was in preparation, but dropped consideration due to opposition that compromised the acceptance of the rest of the Act. The question lay dormant until 1956, when a provi-

sion for making allowances to disabled persons passed
with comparatively little opposition. Enactment of provisions for federal medical aid awaited the new wave of
social reform initiated in the Kennedy-Johnson administration. In that respect, American adoption of welfare
practices deviated sharply from European practices; there
the national welfare systems from the first had provided
means for spreading the risks of illness. The reason for
the delay no doubt arose partly from the fact that the
United States had no extensive system of friendly societies. Even so the reluctance of Americans to adopt even
commercial medical insurance is difficult to account for.
The most important single obstacle was the opposition of
the American Medical Association, which has fiercely
resisted all programs that compromise the principle of
free-enterprise medicine. The AMA has succeeded in
mobilizing in its support Americans' doctrinaire commitment to individualistic practices in general. The shock of
the depression was needed to begin the flight toward collectivism, and even that did not quite suffice to overcome
the opposition of the AMA.

The Professional Guild as Pressure Group

The AMA's opposition to state medical relief has
made it a textbook example of the functioning of pressure
groups as they affect social change. The same situation
exists in other areas, although not with the same intensity.
Let us therefore examine the role of the AMA in medical-
welfare legislation.

A professional guild nowadays may be defined as a
private corporation which society has allowed to assume
the responsibility of overseeing the performance of an
important social function. The key to the power of a guild
is its control over the training and licensing of practition-

ers. The primary purpose for this from the point of view of society is to assure quality control over the qualifications of the practitioners. Admission to the guild is conditional upon fulfilling requirements of training in guild-approved institutions, by apprenticeship, or (as in the case of physicians) by both. The procedures established, however, make it possible also to practice professional "birth control" at several points in the process, as by limiting the number of apprentices, as the skilled construction-workers' unions do; or by certification of training institutions and by licensing provisions, as the medical and bar associations do. Formal membership in the guild may be required, as in the case of construction workers and lawyers admitted to the bar; or it may not be, as in the case of physicians, only a small and diminishing majority of whom are enrolled in the AMA. The essential thing is that the guild asserts control of a social service by virtue of claiming a monopoly of a field of professional expertise — often, as in the case of barbers, a claim with a very dubious basis. In the absence of other influence groups of comparable strength the guild by default can exercise *de facto* control over the whole function. Frequently the guilds can also specify the conditions of labor. Their influence upon the availability of their members' services necessarily also implies influence over the pricing of the services, in accordance with the usual economic laws of supply and demand. Guildsmen rarely engage in price competition, and in some cases, as in those of the crafts unions, outright price control is legally sanctioned.

The American Medical Association, the American Bar Association, and the skilled crafts unions of the AFL type are all guilds of this nature, and in all of those cases serious question has been raised as to the ways in which they discharge the social responsibilities which society has

allowed them to assume. Any extensive program of social
reform will have to deal with that question. The AMA,
since it deals in the matters of personal life and health
which arouse particular anxiety, has been thoroughly examined and has attracted severe criticism. That is somewhat unfair, because the alleged abuses of the AMA are
no greater than those of other professional guilds. Nevertheless it is useful to us as a laboratory example of the
kinds of problems presented by the resistance of professional guilds to social change.

The AMA in Politics before 1960

The AMA played an invaluable role in improving
the poor state of American medicine around the turn of
the century, principally by assuming the social functions
of accrediting training institutions and controlling the
licensing of physicians. Under AMA auspices American
medicine has continued to be among the best in the world.
All institutions in time become ossified, however, and the
AMA has been no exception. In the post-World War II
period medicine has become the most lucrative of the
guilds, conveying the unpleasant implication that physicians have manipulated guild certification procedures to
their own advantage. An epidemic of malpractice suits is
interpreted by some as evidence of a degree of loss of
confidence in the good faith of physicians in protecting
the public interest.

The Great Depression had a considerable effect on
the AMA's politics. Then, unlikely as it seems now, many
physicians were under-employed and in distressed financial circumstances. The situation was particularly galling
to members of the guild which demands the most rigorous
and prolonged training of any craft. In strictly human
terms one cannot blame the physicians for using their

expertise and political leverage to protect their private interests, and for that matter their incomes have increased less than some other categories of medical expense. Nevertheless the outcome has been to make the AMA one of our most jealous guardians of the free-enterprise system. In the thirties it opposed the group practice of medicine, now commonplace and very useful to the physicians who like the system. It also strongly opposed commercial and mutual medical insurance plans, despite the fact that they had functioned very well in Europe for more than a century. In the 1960s the AMA became reconciled to medical insurance only as an alternative to state-supported ("socialized") medicine. The opposition of the AMA has of course inspired opposite and even greater efforts on the part of social welfarists. The overall effect has been to force the AMA into a fighting retreat, accepting in one generation programs that it fought in the preceding. That is not to say that the AMA has no valid arguments; it does. So far federal support of medicine has been extended primarily to the old. Let us therefore examine AMA objections to Medicare as an example of their general arguments.

Objections to Medicare

Part of the debate over Medicare revolved about the real need of the elderly for social assistance. The AMA insisted that the elderly had the financial resources to assure their own care by direct payments, through commercial and nonprofit insurance plans, and by charitable care by the physicians themselves. This led to a re-examination of the financial position of the aged and also caused a re-examination of the coverage and adequacy of commercial, nonprofit, and social insurance programs. The arguments never were reconciled, and in view of the fact

that they ultimately resolved themselves into questions of
the definition of such nebulous terms as "adequacy" and
"need," it is unlikely that they ever could have been. In
the end that aspect of the debate was simply overridden
by the passage of the Medicare amendment to the Social
Security Act.

The AMA early in the debate brought forward an
objection applying to social insurance programs in general,
but not mentioned in other connections. This objection is
that the general thrust of social legislation is to isolate the
aged from the mainstream of society. "They worry less
about health and finances than they do about rejection,"
said an AMA spokesman in 1961. "They are oppressed
with the feeling of not being wanted any longer, of not
being useful, of not being important. They feel that they
have been stripped of their value, and hence of their dignity as human beings." [13] Physicians perhaps have more
insight than social workers do into some problems of the
aged in that they must diagnose ailments of psychic origin
or with a component of psychic sickness. Welfare advocates are apt to emphasize the values that derive from
freeing the children of the aged from financial responsibility for their parents' illnesses. But it is also true that
one of our major social sicknesses today is alienation. There
is no more pitiful manifestation of that alienation than the
isolation and neglect of the aged in their retirement colonies or, worse yet, in nursing homes where they are filed
until death affords release. Legal compulsion to force
mature citizens to support their parents might not be

[13] Quoted in Eugene Feingold, *Medicare: Policy and Politics.
A Case Study and Policy Analysis* (San Francisco: Chandler Publishing Company, 1966), p. 28.

preferable, but certainly no society can take pride in resorting to measures that inevitably encourage such a shunning of responsibility.

The objection to Medicare most ardently pressed by AMA spokesmen was that socially-supported medicine interposes a third party between the physician and patient, thereby disrupting the traditional doctor-patient relationship. That argument has rung a less sympathetic note among welfare advocates. First, it is easy to suspect the physician of pressing the argument because of self-interest; perhaps he simply does not want a third party intervening in financial ways. Despite AMA objections, it is a matter of simple prudence for persons to spread the risks of illness, and it is completely in accord with the free-enterprise tradition to do so at least through voluntary programs. Furthermore, the welfarist points out, the trend of modern medicine toward specialization has already disrupted the physician-patient relationship, and certainly for the better overall, although all must regret the tendency toward further dehumanization of professional services.

What the physician most fears, of course, is that in a socially-regulated medical system the quality of medicine would be degraded. That argument must not be dismissed out of hand. Those most familiar with bureaucracies are most likely to fear that socialized medicine could mean second-class medicine. There is at least one solid piece of evidence to support that fear. In the later 1960s there developed a movement to train physicians' aides, medical practitioners of sub-professional level. The suggestion has its precedent in that the military services have always trained a small proportion of medical corpsmen to administer some medical care while not directly supervised by physicians. Under certain circumstances (such as extended submarine patrols in wartime) their responsibilities may extend well into the areas normally allotted only to fully-qualified physicians.

It is noteworthy that the precedent for this sub-professional practice stems from one of our enclaves of socialized medicine. A private physician could use such an aide only with extreme caution, because under law he is liable to loss of his license and/or a malpractice suit if his aide makes a mistake; but a sovereign government cannot be sued without its own consent. Government-administered medical institutions, that is, are relieved of liabilities that are imposed on private practitioners. The Soviet Union too makes extensive use of sub-professional medical personnel, while by contrast the laws of our states forbid the private practice of medicine by any but the fully-qualified.

The Department of Defense and the Soviet Union both administer a high quality of medical care; therefore we need not assume that socialized medicine automatically means inferior medicine. In our case, however, free-enterprise medicine sets the standards of practice throughout our society. What socialized medicine might mean in an environment lacking the competition of private practitioners, and with the obtuseness to individual needs characteristically shown by large institutions, is a topic worthy of most serious thought.

Advocates of extended welfare simply do not believe that social control of medicine would degrade its quality; and even if those fears were realized, they add, second-class medicine is better than none. AMA spokesmen do not believe such a choice to be necessary, since in their opinion charity and existing public support afford an acceptable standard of medical care to all. Welfare advocates indignantly deny that premise, and there the argument rests in futility.

to the beneficiaries suggest that those fears have some foundation.

The Medicaid program is intended to supply medical care to indigents other than the old. It seeks to rationalize and improve the existing programs of medical support by affording increased federal aid to states that establish "single and improved" medical care programs for needy children and the aged, blind, and disabled. "Medical indigence" can be established for those not entitled to other welfare payments. In New York state "medical indigence" was established at an income level of $4,500 for a family of four, at which level substantially all hospital and doctor bills would be paid. Families with higher incomes receive progressively less support. The promoters of Medicaid hope in the end to see provision of medical care for all.

The Expenses of Socialized Medicine

Opponents of socialized medicine have throughout warned that the costs of the system will be intolerable. The costs of medical care have been rising sharply anyway since 1929, and indeed that is one of the principal reasons for the drive for socialized medicine. Total expenditures rose by 700 percent between 1929 and 1961, and the proportion of GNP devoted to medical costs increased from 3.6 percent in 1929 to 5.7 percent in 1961. Per capita costs rose 146 percent between over those of 1929, and 39 percent above 1948 (all of the above in constant dollars). The major factors in the increase were hospital costs, increased about six times since 1935, and physicians' fees, a little more than doubled. Drug charges have also increased, but by less than half.[14]

[14] Feingold, pp. 4–5.

The proportion of medical expenses for the aged covered by OASDHI is met by a levy of 0.60 percent payroll tax (matched by employers) which is scheduled to rise to 0.90 percent in 1987. In 1967 a total of $3,395,000,000 was disbursed through OASDHI. That was only a small part of the category of all medical care under state and federal public programs; the overall total amounted to $15,878,000,000, about 62 percent from federal funds and the remainder from state and local sources.[15] Government medical aid is already a massive enterprise.

The expenses of socialized medicine obviously will increase sharply, but by how much it is at present impossible to say. By 1969 the OASDHI disbursements for the aged had nearly doubled to $6,598,000,000. The costs of all public support of health and medical care had increased about 42 percent to $22,611,000,000, with the proportion of the cost borne by the federal government rising to 66.9 percent. The programs are not stabilized even yet, however. In 1968 and 1969 the program was still being implemented in a number of states; some states were unable to finance their share of the programs from the tax resources their citizens would vote; the press was reporting cases of flagrant profiteering on the part of some physicians and pharmacists; and an entire new industry of free-enterprise hospitals and nursing homes established by high-flying entrepreneurs was showing the glamour usually attributed to space-age speculative stocks. The program lends itself to some flagrant abuses, but if such abuses were allowed to govern the introduction of social programs social progress would have stopped at the campfire level. The current abuses have nothing to do with the principles of socialized medicine.

[15] *Abstracts,* 1970, pp. 276, 277, Tables 415 and 416.

The larger question is — How will the program work out in the long run? For that we must look to the foreign experience and to the activities of welfare-oriented pressure groups. The latter make no secret of their intention to extend medical care to all sectors of the population as soon as possible; European experience indicates that universal medicare is the predictable goal of evolution. In 1971 the enactment of some comprehensive program appeared to be imminent.

As to the impact on the public in the states that have had medical aid for a long period (in Germany for nearly a century), the program is taken matter-of-factly. Britain has shown more resistance than one might expect, considering that social medical insurance has been in effect since 1911. At times some public dissatisfaction is expressed, but only in matters of detail. There is no appreciable likelihood of abandonment of the program. Many British physicians are opposed to the program, and they are prone to take refuge in the Commonwealth havens for the practice of free-enterprise medicine. Aside from the low-order discontent manifested by the grousing customarily directed at any public service, there is no reason to believe that the British and continental programs are any less successful than other social services.

It seems safest to predict, therefore, that the expenses of socialized medicine will be balanced at the point at which they cost as much as the taxpayer is willing to pay. As with all other public services, it can also confidently be predicted that Medicare will absorb all the money the public will provide.

Unemployment

The most immediate problem that confronted the New Deal was unemployment. Most of the emergency legislation of the first New Deal concerned various schemes for coping with the masses of willing but idle workmen. The problem was by no means an unfamiliar one, as the industrial society always had a proportion of unemployed men. Agrarian societies did too, for that matter, but that was not our problem in the thirties. The recurrent trade depressions had always been marked by increased unemployment, but since they were comparatively shortlived the problem had not been so pressing. Also, as long as the frontier was open it could reasonably be asserted than an able-bodied man could earn his living. The closing of the frontier as well as industrialization therefore affected public attitudes toward unemployment. Agitation for unemployment insurance plans at the state level began as early as 1916; under the pressure of the depression, the first such plan was enacted in Wisconsin in 1932.

A number of other states were considering similar plans, so that by 1934 the administration was compelled to function in an environment in which vested interests were already established. The result was an unemployment assistance program that well illustrates the mix of federal and state responsibility. The program basically covers employees of firms hiring four or more workers; some states extend coverage to firms with only one employee. Benefits were originally financed by a 3 percent payroll tax on the first $3,000 of earnings levied on employers (only two states require contributions by employees). Providing a state has in effect an unemployment compensation program that meets minimum federal specifications, each state may require that employers pay as much as 90 percent of the payroll tax to the state. All states have the appropriate legislation. The combined effect of the federal and state legislation is to establish a state-administered unemployment compensation program financed by a payroll tax originally fixed at 3 percent of the first $3,000 of earnings, with the state taking 2.7 percent and the federal government the remaining 0.3 percent. The federal legislation only establishes a floor on taxation and benefits. The states on their own initiative may expand coverage and benefits and raise either the tax base or the tax rate to finance extended benefits; the state may also raise both. Funds collected are deposited in the Unemployment Trust Fund in the Treasury, where, like the OASDHI funds, they are invested in interest-bearing government securities. A qualified unemployed worker applies for benefits in accordance with state laws which must meet minimum standards determined by federal legislation.

Federal legislation concerning the unemployment insurance program has changed little since enactment of the Social Security Act, and altered circumstances have called into question the adequacy of the program. Federal legislation still provides for a wage base of $3,000, and the base rate of taxation has been increased by only 0.1 percent; the increase goes to the Treasury to provide for increased costs of administration. The $3,000 wage base in 1938 represented a ratio of 98 percent of total wages, but by 1963 the proportion had slipped to 58.1 percent of total wages. Disturbed by the inadequacy of the coverage, by 1964 fourteen states had raised the taxable wage base. The influence of local conditions was illustrated by the fact that twelve contiguous states raised their wage base into the range of $3,300 to $4,200; while the two detached states, Alaska and Hawaii, with atypical economies, respectively raised the base to $7,200 and to 90 percent of average annual wage. Furthermore, in 1964 thirty-one states had employer tax rates in effect above the 2.7 percent minimum. The range was from 3.0 percent to 7.2 percent, but in only two states did the rate exceed 4.6 percent.[16]

Uneasiness as to the adequacy of the program impels an expansion of coverage and taxation, but the competition between states affords incentive for keeping the rates low. Also, within the same state some employers have a tax advantage due to the operation of the "experience rating" system allowed by many states, whereby employers with stable employment records may have their tax burdens reduced and in some cases eliminated. That tends to shift the unemployment tax burden onto newly-established businesses. As the program slips increasingly out of correspondence with contemporary conditions, the question arises as to whether the program is financed well enough to stabilize the income of the unemployed at present economic levels.

The program is also very incomplete in its coverage. In many states employees of small firms are not covered, nor are employees of state and local governments, those in agricultural employment, domestic workers, and some other categories. Those who are covered may be disqualified for benefits, including those unable or unwilling to work, those who quit without cause, those involved in labor disputes, and others. The number disqualified is substantial; in 1954 it amounted to 1,616,000 of the cov-

[16] William Haber and Merrill G. Murray, *Unemployment Insurance in the American Economy: An Historical Review and Analysis* (Homewood, Illinois: Richard D. Irwin, Inc., 1966), pp. 360–363.

ered workers.[17] The benefits are payable only after a period of ineligibility and are limited to a maximum period that varies up to 26 weeks. Finally, the weekly benefits are widely variable between states, ranging from a low of $26.46 in Mississippi to $50.45 in California.[18]

We may note that the financing of the unemployment program differs from that of OASDHI in that it does not involve contributory payments by the employee. His "rights" to unemployment compensation therefore are dependent upon the judgment of administrative agencies.

The program has built into it a number of problems which could become serious under some circumstances. First is that it reflects a balance between the conflicting goals of relieving destitution while maintaining work incentive. It provides for state initiative under federal supervision. It affords advantages to business firms and states that stabilize employment which can easily be converted into competitive advantages. Perhaps most important is the fact that the plan did not come into effect until 1938, when the depression was shortly to be ended by the war. Employment was high then and has remained high since, so that the trust funds were able to accumulate large reserves. The tax base therefore could be held low and some employers could be partially or wholly relieved of the tax liability. The program has never really been put to the test of widespread unemployment. The British unemployment relief system in the 1920s proved unequal to its task. Enacted in 1911, it had not as yet built up an adequate reserve by 1920 and was soon bankrupted by the onset of depression. Their benefits exhausted during the 1920s,

[17] Helen I. Clarke, *Social Legislation,* 2nd ed. (New York: Appleton-Century-Crofts, 1957), p. 634.

[18] *Abstracts,* 1968, p. 294. The lowest payment is $19.69 in Puerto Rico, but its economy is atypical.

British laborers had to rely on a dole through much of the 1930s. The Roosevelt administration's legislative proposal was designed with the British experience in mind. The program enacted provides adequately for those covered, but the coverage is incomplete at best and there is reason to doubt that it could meet the test of widespread depression.

Special and General Assistance

Programs of "special" assistance are those which aid the blind and disabled, and include the highly controversial program for Aid to Families with Dependent Children (AFDC). "General" assistance, as the name suggests, provides for relief of destitution not covered by specific programs. Stemming from the Poor Laws, the common feature of the programs is that they afford the elasticity to accommodate the social debris not otherwise protected: the handicapped, derelicts, vagabonds, indigent migrants, the aged having no rights to public or private pensions, the great catchall of miserables whose claim rests on the appeal to human sympathy rather than to any right established by law or by the prevailing ethic of economic liberalism. They are the ones who in all of nature outside of human society would go under in the Darwinian struggle for survival. Nineteenth-century social Darwinists argued that it was to the benefit of mankind that they should be permitted to die off.

The possibility of disposing of unwanted dependents must not be entirely discounted. It is true that there are very few instances of societies that dispose of dependents past the age of infancy, and then only in the most extreme circumstances. On the other hand, infanticide and abortion (which may be viewed as pre-parturition infanticide) are rather common. Oddly enough, disposal of dependents is becoming popular in the most prosperous lands with the spread of abortion upon demand of the mother. A strong drive for the legalization of abortion in the United States developed during the 1960s. Most of the reasons put forward for the legalization do not bear dispassionate examination. Over-population hardly applies; our population density is less than one-fifth even of the major European lands. Nor is there a compelling economic motive; a curious feature of the present abortion drive is that it occurs at the peak of our economic prosperity. Other reasons advanced lie in rather nebulous realms such as concern for the welfare of other nations or the right of a woman to control the use of her body — which of course does not include her right to control the bodies of others. Many physicians who have to confront desperate women naturally favor legalized abortion, and some are refreshingly frank in admitting that they view it as a necessary back-up for failures of contraceptive measures. While the other reasons mentioned are not wholly invalid, we can justifiably conclude that we are confronted with the curious prospect of the disposal of unwanted dependents on a massive scale, not because of economic necessity, but in large part merely as a matter of convenience. This argument is in no way directed either for or against the legalization of abortion; it is intended to cut through the fog of rationalizations surrounding the issue, to lay bare some of the little-discussed motivations of the drive for legalization, and thereby to illustrate the fact that disposal of one category of dependents is becoming an accepted practice.

From that consideration alone the miscellaneous dependents in our society might fear for their physical safety, but human experience indicates that there is no serious likelihood that competitive social Darwinism will be allowed to operate further. Since the dependents are not to be disposed of, they must be cared for. The distinctive feature of this category of welfare programs is that they stemmed from Old Poor Law practices, which in the 1930s were supplemented by grants in aid from the federal government. In many ways general assistance still resembles Poor Law provisions more than one might expect.

Settlement, American Style

The first problem is that of settlement, which answers the question, "Who is to be responsible for the care of this dependent?" Settlement depends upon residence in a particular state, and often also upon residence within jurisdictions of each state. About three-fourths of the states have legislation authorizing intrastate removal, and half provide for interstate removal. More than one-half of the states formerly also provided for exclusion of indigents, but exclusion lost its constitutional basis in 1941 with a U. S. Supreme Court decision forbidding the state of California to exclude indigents. The majority opinion held that exclusion was an unconstitutional burden upon interstate commerce; Justice William O. Douglas in a concurring opinion held that exclusion was an unconstitutional limitation upon freedom of movement.[19] The effect of the decision was to open the way for the indigent to seek the highest level of welfare payment available providing only that he could somehow survive during the mandatory residence period required to obtain settlement. The result has been an influx of indigents into areas with generous welfare policies, notably New York City. Mayor John V. Lindsay therefore has some problems in common with

[19] Clarke, pp. 510–512.

Gaius Gracchus. It is to be hoped that he will escape the same fate.

There is also a substantial movement to eliminate residence requirements altogether. The constitutional basis of settlement legislation is under attack, and some federal welfare legislation forbids states to impose residence requirements for beneficiaries of some federally-financed programs. The pattern suggests the impending adoption of a national settlement such as evolved in nineteenth-century Britain, with a corresponding centralization of direction of welfare services. The abolition of settlement is attractive to many who favor radical extension of welfare services. In its most extreme form the argument constitutes a demand that society afford the economic resources as a matter of right to any person to move wheresoever he pleases without regard to responsibility for his own support. That view of settlement therefore again raises the philosophical question of individual responsibility.

Aid to Families with Dependent Children

The federal contribution to this important program is also provided for by the Social Security Act. It falls into a distinctive category for several reasons. First, the welfare of the young always strikes a peculiarly sympathetic note, for it is a part of the Christian ethic that the dependent child and its mother are entitled to support. This does not preclude their neglect and even their exploitation, but their abuse is regarded as especially unjustifiable. Programs ostensibly to improve their conditions of life initially afforded the rationale for improving the conditions of life and labor of the poor in general. Too, all other general assistance programs are intended to alleviate the

worst miseries of the unfortunate and constitute more or
less hopeless attempts to salvage something from the human wreckage of the social system; it has been nearly two
centuries since a Utopian could dream that paupers could
be made a social asset. Only in children can hope be seen
of salvaging a considerable class of dependents and even
of breaking the cycle of poverty which too often con-
demns successive generations of the same family to lives
of misery.

There is agreement that the AFDC program encourages men to abandon their families. Fathers who cannot
obtain work are thrown upon the resources of general
assistance (outside of the unemployment security provisions, for usually they have never had regular employment). AFDC payments cannot be made to such families.
If the father abandons them, a mouth is removed from
the household, which automatically increases the standard
of living for the remaining family. The mother becomes
eligible for AFDC payments, which usually are higher
than the general assistance payments the father could get.
Everything therefore favors abandonment as the best
means available to the unemployed poor man for supplying his family. If adopted deliberately, that social manipulation would be a credit to the ingenuity of its inventor,
though not to his humanity.

It is not possible, and if it were possible it would not
be humane, to prevent the mother from entertaining other
men. This virtually dictates that some of the women will
continue to produce children, and opens the program to
criticism that it encourages the breeding of bastards as a
sort of "employment" on the part of women who wish to
perpetuate their dependency as a way of life. The charge
is an ancient one; bastardy was believed to be as prevalent
in eighteenth-century England as it is here and now, and

was viewed as dimly. The charge of deliberate bastardy is probably unfounded in most cases. In the fall of 1970 the largest AFDC payment that could be made in Little Rock, Arkansas, was $141.00 per month for a mother with seven children, a scale hardly likely to encourage the production of further unwanted children. Rather what is involved is the entrapment of persons in a way of life that they themselves see as undesirable, but to which they have become accustomed as a blind man may become accustomed to his disability, and from which they lack the personal resources to escape. Money, training, and other assistance help some to escape; but the questionable success of the various programs of the War on Poverty has taught us the extreme difficulty of dealing with the residue of the poverty-stricken that remain with us, even in the case of children.

The advocates of extended welfarism deny that there is anything alarming in the situation except for the inadequate level of AFDC payments and the poor conditions of slum life. They would increase rather than diminish AFDC payments so as to afford a really comfortable standard of living, open creches for the care of infants so that mothers might work if they chose (but not apply economic compulsion to work), and improve homes and schools. Their argument is that the poverty of those on AFDC reflects the social pathology of the well-to-do rather than of the abandoned family. They would cure not the poor who, they believe, are not responsible for their poverty, but the rich, who are. Once more that argument carries us into the realm of consideration of social philosophy.

State Responsibility: Education

There are two programs which are half or nearly half funded by the states: "other" social welfare, a catch-all, and medical care, for which the major burden of expenses is rapidly shifting to the social insurance system. The major welfare program for which states are almost wholly responsible is the massive educational system, which at $35.6 billion accounts for over one-third of our total governmental welfare expenditures. Eighty-five percent of the funds are raised and expended by the states. Only the total social insurance program exceeds it in magnitude, and no other welfare program amounts to one-third of the education expenditures.

We are not accustomed to thinking of education as a welfare program. Indeed, most of us probably are not accustomed to thinking at all about its basic purposes, even though the subject of "what is wrong with our schools" is one of our favorite topics of conversation. Our system was established in the nineteenth century; since then it has been accepted rather uncritically as a good thing, and most of our attention has been devoted to doing a better job of giving a traditional education to an ever-increasing proportion of the population. That the original purposes may no longer be valid, or that the system may not be serving them, has been forcefully drawn to our attention by some college students of the 1960s. There is evidence on every hand that our educational system needs reform, and reform generally has to begin with a redefinition of the purposes which the institution is intended to serve. One approach to such a reexamination is to consider education as an institution intended to promote the welfare of the whole society and/or the individual. This is not the place for a full examination of all functions of education. Only the functions relating to social conditioning, preparation for productivity, and relief of unemployment will be considered.

Social conditioning of its subjects, so as better to enable them to serve the purposes of the community, is the basic function of every educational system. The sixteenth-century Jesuits operated missionary schools in order to make better Catholics of their pupils; seventeenth-century Calvinists in Massachusetts, to make better Puritans of them; twentieth-century Nazis, to make better Aryans of them; the Soviets, to make New Soviet Men of them; in recent America, "to educate them for citizenship"; and some contemporary social critics seek to use the schools as devices for conditioning the young to be socially-oriented rather than individualistic. Insofar as all of those systems have the goal of conditioning the social behavior of their subjects, none are morally preferable to the others. Morality is irrelevant. If any society is to function, its members must be willing to subordinate themselves to some degree to its dictates; historically, our society has merely tried to minimize the social demands. The most important agency for social conditioning is the family; the school is the strongest secondary agency up to the age of puberty; the peer-group contends for ascendancy in the adolescent years, and achieves ascendancy when the pupil leaves the shelter of the school for participation in the outside world. We too often think of our school systems in isolation from the environment. In a lifetime of experience school is only one institution for social conditioning, albeit by far the most important formal institution.

Social conditioning is generally accomplished in the first six to eight years of schooling. That time suffices also (or at least should suffice) to impart basic communication and computational skills needed for the operation of a modern, industrially-oriented social system. Insofar as those are welfare functions, they affect the welfare of the whole community, not that of the individual alone. In fact, the conditioning may even be harmful to the individual in some cases, as when it conditions him to accept military service at the expense of his life or health. Since social conditioning is intended to benefit the whole community, it is reasonable to expect the community to bear the costs.

Preparation for productivity benefits both the community and the individual. Society must have certain proportions of carpenters, pilots, teachers, accountants, physicians, and so on, to fill the roles in the intricately-articulated configuration of the social network. The individual is motivated to learn those roles by the usual complex of motivations — the whip, the carrot, and perhaps instinct. In most of the debates over poverty problems through the ages the assumption has been that work is motivated by the whip of the need to earn a living and by the carrot of the desire to earn a *good* living or to acquire wealth. It has generally been assumed that, while work may be an ethical good in itself, it is inherently unpleasant and that some positive social sanction must be applied to induce productivity. Since about the turn of the twentieth century, however, it has been pointed out by some that work can also be a pleasure. This is becoming increasingly true with the advance of the industrial revolution, which first freed man from gruelling manual labor and now promises to liberate him from the worst routine of the factory. As industrialization advances "work," while as time-consuming and demanding as ever, may increasingly capitalize on man's play instinct, creativity, curiosity, and similar undefinable but well-recognized drives.

There is considerable difference of opinion as to whether society or the individual benefits most from train-

ing for productivity, and as "work" becomes more pleasant the difference of opinion can be expected to grow.
Socially-oriented persons assert that the whole social
group benefits by the activity of all, therefore no particular
individual is more important than others, and consequently unequal sharing of production is unjustified. Some
varieties of socialists believe that a person could reasonably be expected to work as an architect in the morning
and as a hod-carrier in the afternoon; there should be no
status or compensation differences between the roles. Such
a view is the natural consequence of a "social forces" interpretation of history, of which the Marxists are an extreme
example. Individualists argue that each man should be
free to seek his own destiny; therefore it is the individual
who profits most from his enterprise, and he should be
expected to bear the costs of his conditioning. He should
regard those costs as an investment from which a rather
handsome return can be expected. This yet again raises
the larger philosophical question of collectivism versus
individualism. We shall cut the discussion short at this
point with the observation that, without much reflection
on the matter, Americans have decided that virtually all
kinds of education are to be accomplished at community
expense. Charges are made only at the college level if at
all, and in no case cover more than a fraction of the costs.

Relief of unemployment logically should be an end-
product of conditioning for productivity, which has been
regarded as the principal means of curing poverty ever
since Queen Elizabeth's Poor Law provided for apprenticing of parish wards. Those provisions have been updated
through the centuries with the advance of civilization.
Colonial America was in the forefront of the movement to
extend education to all, and this country remains so to
this day. In view of our almost mystical reverence for

anything that can be labeled "education" it is no wonder that it remains a mainstay of our anti-poverty programs. That reliance has, however, coincided with a virtual collapse of the educational system precisely where it is most needed, in the slum districts of our largest cities. Three causes for the breakdown which are particularly pertinent to our consideration of poverty problems can be suggested: the confusion as to objectives for the educational system, the use of the schools as detention institutions for restricting the labor market, and the operation of diminishing returns on investment.

The confusion as to objectives is rather obvious. Much of the confusion stems from the failure to distinguish between the functions of social conditioning and conditioning for productivity. One consequence is that most high schools have a college-preparatory liberal arts curriculum, despite the fact that only about half of their graduates ever enter college and half of those can't or don't stay. To many impoverished youngsters whose immediate needs are for the jobs by which they can earn good incomes such curricula can seem wholly irrelevant. The public vocational schools have dealt with only a small proportion of students and, having been regarded as low-prestige institutions, have been avoided as much as possible. (A recent emphasis on vocational education may be changing that situation.) It is taken more or less for granted that the minimum qualification for employment is a high school diploma, and the youth without one is handicapped in obtaining employment whether or not the high school curriculum is pertinent to the needs of a particular job. It is possible to concede that in the long run the liberal arts curriculum offers the greatest value for life enrichment, and yet to recognize that it is difficult to convince a poverty-stricken youth of its relevance when his immediate needs are earthier. It might be helpful to reorder the priorities of education according to immediacy, satisfying the stomach first and then the heart and mind.

The function of the schools as detention institutions is rarely commented upon today. References can be found to this purpose in some of the very early writings of the labor movement. The movement urged universal, free, and compulsory education at the time when labor was struggling to improve its competitive position by restricting or eliminating the labor of women and children. The workingmen's primary concern was for the welfare of the young; but human motivation is rarely simple, and there were some ulterior motives as well. One was that the labor leaders wished through the spread of literacy to make the laboring class more accessible to their written propaganda, and still another motive was to restrict the labor market. By the time of the Great Depression laws were in effect severely restricting the labor of youth under eighteen and forbidding it in some occupations. The youth's occupation is supposed to be attendance at school, whether or not he wants to be there or sees any relevance in the curriculum.

The detention function may well have much to do with the constant lengthening of the educational process. If one accepts our twelve-year system at face value, it would appear that we operate on the assumption that if eight years of school are good, twelve are 50 percent better and sixteen twice as good. The high-school diploma became the socially-accepted minimum certificate of education by mid-century; today two-year community colleges are flourishing and dismay is often expressed that "only" half of the high-school graduates enter college and that so many drop out before obtaining degrees. The general tone of much of the discussion of the educational system seems to be that more is better. There are of course many reasons for such an attitude, but one of them is the uneasiness sometimes expressed at the accentuation of the unemployment problem if the youth were not occupied in school.

The requirement laid on our public schools to accept nearly all the youth except the mentally or physically handicapped, no matter how ill-adapted or ill-motivated, naturally has pernicious side-effects. It becomes nearly impossible for the educator to resist pressures to promote the student even when his learning is manifestly deficient. As a result, many a classroom has its group of "students" who exist on a live-and-let-live basis with their teachers. The tacit bargain is that they will receive a diploma at the age of eighteen on condition that they stay off the streets, stay off unemployment rolls, and stay out of prison. The diploma awarded does not necessarily certify much as to their learning. A high proportion of college freshmen are functionally illiterate — they can pass literacy tests, but do not know how to use printed matter even as sources of information storage and retrieval, let alone as sources of pleasure and enlightenment. In addition to a high school diploma, most American colleges today require for admission an acceptable score on the American College Testing program (ACT) tests or some equivalent.

Though not related to public education, we may note here the similar drive of labor movements further to restrict the labor market by the forced retirement of workers at the age of 60 and even 55. To tell hundreds of thousands of able-bodied men of 55 that they aren't needed any more raises frightening possibilities.

The award of a high school diploma therefore for many is a meaningless rite of passage. The implications of this state of affairs for the cure of poverty are ominous. The question asked by life is "What can you do?" A person can achieve a certain status within his peer group simply as a human being, but if anything the world now has entirely too many human beings in it. Human currency is being debased by oversupply. The person of value *in* a community is one who is of value *to* the community. In twentieth-century America, like it or not, the only way of becoming a valuable person is through *effective* education — in the long run, fulfilling meaningless nominal requirements will not serve.

A factor complicating the use of education as a cure for poverty is that the effectiveness of schools pretty accurately reflects the general conditions of the communities they serve. Poor communities breed poor schools, and the schools are poor almost without regard to the money put into them. Nevertheless, it is also true that the same slum schools now described as blackboard jungles were once quite good enough to enable thousands of German, Irish, and Jewish immigrants to enter the affluent suburbs. That is no recommendation for the perpetuation of slum schools. Millions of immigrants worked their way out of the slums, but other millions didn't. There is no reason to perpetuate challenges which cannot be overcome by a large proportion of humanity. But neither is there any reason to doubt that the educational system, even in its present unsatisfactory form, can continue to afford the avenue for escape from those conditions.

It is also a fact, however, that for any specified aptitude some persons will be wholly inept, and apparently some persons have no aptitudes of value to the community. Translated into expenditures for education, that means that for any specified goal of education, the expenses of educating each individual rise as one descends on the aptitude curve until a point is reached at which the expenses rise very sharply. The extreme is reached in cases of physical, mental, or character cripples for whom no techniques

exist for making them socially useful. Realistically, so long
as the community requires allocation of production according to priorities, the point of diminishing returns will be
fixed at the point at which the community concludes that
custodial care of the inept is preferable to further expenses
to make them useful. Such decisions are rarely expressed
explicitly. Tacit and often unconscious motives govern the
social action. This again brings us face-to-face with the
universal and never-solved question of what to do with the
human being who is socially incompetent. The problem
has been grave enough in the past. As the definition of
"incompetence" is fixed at progressively higher levels, due
to the increasing sophistication required of citizens in an
industrialized and automated social system, the question
will become ever more pressing. Still again, that falls
within the province of the larger social question.

Liberal education requires only a mention in order to
round out the picture, since by definition it is non-voca-
tional and therefore not directly related to the immediate
problem of reclaiming individuals from poverty. Vocational training teaches us how to do things of value; liberal
education helps us learn to decide what things are of value,
what things should be done. It cultivates the faculty of
judgment, which ultimately depends upon the totality of
the life experience of the individual. There is absolutely
no reason to believe that judgment can only be cultivated
between the ages of eighteen and twenty-two, and only
within the framework of the institution socially defined as
a "college." An argument can be made in favor of shifting
emphasis toward vocational training for the young (medicine, law, and similar high-prestige occupations would be
considered vocations and included therein); and opening
institutions for liberal education to all persons so that they
might return at intervals during their lives when they per-

sonally feel the need to reinforce their life experiences by suitable academic education. It is not appropriate to speculate on the results of such an approach in this context.

Why the War on Poverty?

In view of the prevailing prosperity it seems paradoxical that the United States again became preoccupied with the problem of poverty in the 1960s. Certainly there was no particular domestic crisis that precipitated the debate. Apparently the most significant factors in the renewal of interest were the economic prosperity, the international situation, and the flourishing of the civil rights movement.

The economic situation had been grim enough in the 1930s, when the Social Security Act was passed. Any such far-reaching social reform required a lengthy test of its effectiveness. The onset of war diverted attention from internal problems, and also alleviated one of the most pathetic manifestations of poverty by affording employment in war industries to surplus labor. There were many who feared the return of depression when the war should end. Former vice-president Henry A. Wallace, for example, strongly urged government action to guarantee the provision of sixty million jobs.

Despite such alarmism the economy continued to recover from the ravages of war and depression. The wealth of the community as measured by the Gross National Product (GNP) increased phenomenally. By 1960 both the GNP and total personal expenditures had more than doubled over 1940 figures, as measured in constant dollars. Per capita income increased nearly 54 percent between those years. For the generation raised in the depression and anxious to advance the economy, there was good reason for feelings of relief and even of complacency.

There was indeed a good deal of complacency in the Eisenhower years; but mixed with it was also a good deal of uneasiness manifested by such things as the popularity of a novel, *The Man in the Gray Flannel Suit*, the title of which for a time became a symbol of the soul-searching of the well-to-do middle class in questioning its own values. So far as poverty was concerned, one might conjecture that the middle class was caught up in that aspect of the Christian ethic that makes (relatively) wealthy persons feel guilty in the presence of poverty. In any case, the Social Security Act had been in effect long enough not only to have had a full test, but also to have slipped somewhat out of correspondence with current needs. The time was approaching for re-examination of the welfare system.

The easing of international tensions may have encouraged the public to shift its attention more to domestic affairs. The need for reconstructing the economies of the free world states after the ravages of depression and war, and the possibility of nuclear and thermonuclear war with the Soviet Union, preoccupied public attention in the later 1940s and 1950s. By the end of the Eisenhower administration the United States possessed enough bombardment force to do all the damage to the Soviet Union that could be done by bombardment. The Soviet capability was the same. The Soviets tested Kennedy first at Berlin, and then in the Cuban missile crisis. In the latter case the powers were brought eyeball-to-eyeball in a thermonuclear confrontation. Both sides blinked. There is little doubt that at least a tacit bargain was struck. The outcome was the conclusion that no *rational* decision-maker could opt for thermonuclear war. That relieved the public of the worst fears of a catastrophe in comparison with which such skirmishes as Vietnam pale into insignificance. For

the first time in a generation Americans were free to worry
about domestic problems. Worry they did, and with a
vengeance. The rhetoric outdid even that of the 1930s,
when objective conditions were incomparably more difficult.

Another factor contributing to the renewed interest
in social welfare, and contributing most to the heat of the
arguments, was the parallel surgence of a civil rights drive.
The nearest thing to a truly revolutionary situation that
can be found in the United States arises from the race
question, the greatest curse of American society. There is
no necessary connection between the problems of poverty
and race; two-thirds of the persons drawing welfare payments are white. True, this means that there are three
times as many Negroes on welfare as there should be in
proportion to their share of the population and that they
similarly reflect a lower economic status at each level of
society above the poverty line. Nevertheless poverty is
obviously a problem mainly affecting whites, and in many
cases, as in Appalachia, affecting such rugged Americans
as the descendants of Daniel Boone and Davy Crockett.
So far in this book the race question has been ignored as
much as possible so as to avoid an unnecessary and undesirable connection between the two problems. The connection, however, seems to be unavoidable in explaining
the passions aroused by the poverty question in the 1960s.

The 1960s saw a cresting of one of the waves of agitation for extension of civil rights. The previous wave had
begun in the Roosevelt administration, partly as a reaction
to the doctrinaire racism of the 1920s. All administrations
since Roosevelt's had exerted constant pressure to relieve
blacks of their civil disabilities, although the degree of
pressure fluctuated. A full generation had elapsed; it seems
that with the emergence of a majority of Negroes from

conditions of poverty and with the cultivation in them of middle-class abilities and value systems there has developed a really substantial proportion of Negroes who will no longer tolerate an inferior social status. Their attitude is completely in accord with the Puritan ethic engrained in most blacks. A tremendous reservoir of hostility has of course built up over the past three centuries; and the conditions were ripe for a coalition of the abler and more aggressive Negroes together with their doctrinaire white supporters to renew the drive for elimination of their remaining civil disabilities. Again, the easing of the most dangerous of international tensions cleared the way for consideration of domestic problems. In general, it appears that the major problems of the new civil rights movement arise from the fact that legal disabilities are disappearing. Some black leaders are complaining that there is already so much civil rights legislation on the books that much of it is lying unused. The principal problem lies in the hearts of the dominant social group; the white society can be forced not to impose legal liabilities on Negroes, but cannot be forced to love them or accept them socially.

The same doctrinaire groups which pressed against poverty conditions were also those in doctrinaire commitment to the elimination of racism. Consequently there has been a tendency to link the questions of poverty and race, especially when distinguished Negroes such as Martin Luther King, Jr., spoke to both issues. A dramatic example of agitation against poverty-racism was the Poor People's Campaign (PPC) and the establishment of Resurrection City in the spring of 1968. The PPC assumed even greater importance and impact than it otherwise would have in the aftermath of King's assassination.

King himself saw the dangers in linking the poverty

and race questions and purported to speak for *all* of the
poor. It has since been alleged that the Poor People's Campaign was a multi-racial movement.[20] It was not. It was a
movement of Negroes and other minorities. Nearly all of
the whites in Resurrection City were ministers, social
workers, artists, and professors and students (mainly of
sociology). That is, they were conscience-stricken white
middle-class neo-liberals in comfortable economic circumstances. The few old-time white veterans of anti-poverty
and civil rights movements in attendance were dismayed
by the identification of the PPC with the race question,
fearing that racism would be mobilized against measures
to relieve poverty in general.

Those fears were perhaps not justified, principally
because official Washington viewed the Poor People's
Campaign with an imperturbability worthy of the British
Establishment. Neither in formulation nor execution of
programs did the PPC have a perceptible direct effect.
Indeed, if Washington had had the best will in the world
it could not have gratified the desires of the PPC, for the
only program the participants could present was the millenarian demand to end poverty *now*, and don't bother
with details. The nearest thing to concrete demands made
at Resurrection City were for a Guaranteed Annual Income (GAI) and for the government to become the
employer of last resort. The GAI had already been bruited
about for some time, but America has still made no doc-

---

[20] For example, by Michael Harrington, who described Resurrection City as "nonviolent, integrated, committed to democratic
change." See "The Will To Abolish Poverty," *Saturday Review*, 51
(July 27, 1968), p. 41. His description is fair enough except for
integration. The contrary view that follows is based on my observations.

trinaire commitment to that program. Aside from that, the War on Poverty was already functioning but had not had a reasonable opportunity to prove itself.

The War on Poverty

Throughout the 1950s it had never been denied that we still had the poor with us, but they were distinctly a minority of the population, a considerable improvement over the depression era. Furthermore, as measured by objective criteria the poor apparently constituted a declining minority. This last statement, to be sure, concerns a passionately-debated issue which we shall consider in some detail in the next pages; most statisticians would agree that the statement is fair enough as it stands. Yet by the beginning of the 1960s charges were brought that not merely a few but many Americans lived in poverty. It was asserted that anywhere from twenty to forty percent of the population was living in "poverty," "destitution," or "deprivation." The numbers given by welfare advocates were rarely less than 20 million poor and ranged as high as 70 million. The three books most influential in setting the tone of the argument were John Kenneth Galbraith's *The Affluent Society* (1957, rev. ed. 1969), which purported to present a rational as well as an ethical argument for equalization of distribution; Michael Harrington's *The Other America* (1964), an impassioned exposition of neo-millenarianism; and Leon Keyserling's *Progress or Poverty* (1964), which purported to present statistical support for charges of the existence of large numbers of the poor. These and related theses will be examined in some detail at the beginning of Part III. Here we will consider only the form and effect of the poverty programs they inspired.

Upon being elected president in 1960 John F. Kennedy declared that the existence of poverty did not befit a wealthy and powerful state and vowed to do away with it. At the time his statements were taken as fulfilling conventional American political rituals, and there is no particular reason to believe that to be more or less true of him than of other politicians. His ideas on the poverty problem seem to have been crystallized by a *New Yorker* magazine article reviewing a number of books on poverty, with particular attention to Harrington's.[21] In the fall of 1963 Kennedy presented a legislative program intended to alleviate some poverty problems. His proposals found heavy sledding in a Democratic but lukewarm congress. We are now prone to remember Kennedy in the sentimental afterglow of his tragic death, but in the fall of 1963 the best that was being said of him was that he had dealt well with the Cuban missile crisis. His poverty program was in deep trouble at the time of his assassination.

We lack the perspective as yet fully to assess the adminstration of Lyndon Baines Johnson. It seems fairly certain that the public attitude toward his poverty program was affected by popular impressions of Johnson as a person. He had initially attracted national attention in connection with his first senatorial campaign in 1948. The election was contested and decided by an 87-vote majority that almost certainly involved corruption on both sides. In the Senate he performed invaluable functions as majority leader, cultivating a rare reputation as a manipulator of the political system. A contender for the nomination for president in 1960, his credentials were much more impressive than Kennedy's, but he never lost the taint of being a political manipulator, an *unprincipled* politician. There is little objective reason to believe that to be any

[21] *New Yorker*, 38 (January 19, 1963): 82.

more true of Johnson than of most other professional politicians. Neither is there any doubt of the sincerity of his
personal desire to aid the poor. The effect of the climate of
opinion in which he moved, however, was to make it
impossible for large segments of the public really to believe him to be sincere in promoting the poverty program,
which was widely viewed as a patronage device. Since
many politicians of all persuasions did so use the program,
there was ample support for the views of those who regarded it with suspicion. It was in that unpromising climate of opinion that the grandiloquently-named "War on
Poverty" was introduced.

The Economic Opportunity Act

The War on Poverty (WOP) was implemented by
the Economic Opportunity Act. President Kennedy had
made a commitment to include anti-poverty provisions in
his legislative proposals for 1964. Upon assuming office
President Johnson pressed ahead aggressively with the
Kennedy program. The bill was presented to Congress on
16 March 1964 and was signed into law on 20 August.
That was rather brief consideration for such an important
and complex piece of legislation; but some of the most
important provisions, such as those concerning vocational
training, were already familiar to Congress from earlier
legislation. There is no reason to believe that the bill was
ill-considered, except perhaps for the provisions concerning the Community Action Program (CAP). Intended by
the lawmakers as a device to keep southern politicians
honest, the CAP was widely misinterpreted as a Magna
Charta for the poor to administer their own relief funds, a
misconception which contributed to what one commenta-
tor has described as the "maximum feasible misunderstanding" of the program.

The first purpose of the Economic Opportunity Act is to coordinate existing welfare programs, thereby making them more effective, and in some cases to redirect them more specifically for the benefit of the poor. For example, it is a surprise to many to learn that the food-commodities program is provided for under legislation intended primarily to support agricultural farm prices. Insofar as it is a welfare program at all it is intended in the first instance to benefit farmers rather than the poor. The free or cheap distribution of food (as in the days of the Gracchi) is counter-productive for agriculture insofar as it affects the "free-market" prices for farm products. An important function of the EOA is to tilt the balance of the commodities program more toward the benefit of the poor — which also accounts for the persistence of the very awkward device of the food-stamp program, the primary purpose of which is to maintain farm prices.

The two fields in which some originality might be claimed were those of the local coordination of poor relief, and in two special areas of education. We will limit our detailed consideration of WOP provisions to those.

The Community Action Program (CAP)

The most distinctive program of the WOP, the CAP, is directed toward mobilization of the efforts of the poor themselves on their own behalf. The program is based on the assumption that the poor are capable of managing their own affairs, and indeed that pauperization is the natural consequence of paternalism; therefore funds and expert advice should be made available to them to enable them to improve their own lives. Existing programs such as the food-stamp program were to be mobilized and re-directed to the relief of the poor in locally-coordinated programs, and additional funds were to be made available directly through the War on Poverty program, if necessary by-passing local political authorities who sought to use the program for patronage or who proved to be uncooperative.

The CAP came under heavy attack on both doctrinaire and practical grounds. The doctrinaire opponents of the program declared it false to assume that the poor could manage their own affairs: to be poor in a period of unprecedented prosperity was *prima facie* evidence of unfitness to cope with modern life, and money given to them to administer would simply be wasted. Furthermore, many of the CAP activities such as voter registration drives were held to be subversive to social order; it was believed by some that government funds were being used to finance revolutionary activities, and the rhetorical question was asked as to whether any government should be expected to finance those who sought its own overthrow. Such attitudes were reinforced by some CAP programs, such as presentation of the plays of LeRoi Jones, which were deliberately offensive to the white middle class. And finally, City Hall everywhere resented the incursion of alien activities upon their terrain. As a purely practical matter the local CAP centers could not for long avoid the necessity to cooperate with local political authorities.

Despite a good deal of rhetoric about the intention to do away with poverty, the CAP was never very generously financed. We must keep in mind that a total of over $100 billion annually was already spent on all welfare programs. Most of those funds were not directed to the benefit of the poor; but already in 1964 over $13 billion was expended on federal relief specifically for them, in addition to the public services such as education which they share. The figure rose to nearly $24 billion in 1968. Since a function of the CAP was to rationalize and direct the expenditure of some of those funds, its financing cannot be judged solely by its own budget. Nevertheless the appropriation of about $2.5 billion of federal money and about $0.5 billion of non-federal money in the four years 1965–1968 amounted to only about $97 per poor person for the period. Even those funds were unevenly distributed: the CAP grants to the ten cities receiving the most money ranged from a low of $93 per poor person (New York) to a high of $276 (Pittsburgh). Allocation apparently was dependent upon having "the most effective organization and sophistication in the art of grantsmanship." [22]

How effective is the CAP? As yet, no supportable answer can be given. It has been in effect for only five years and most judgments on it reflect opinions the judges already held. It has only one novel feature: the assumption that life's losers, who in a period of unprecedented prosperity still find themselves poor, can nevertheless manage very complex affairs. Really, they have not been permitted to do so. Despite the oratory of the public-relations releases, the centers are essentially under the direction of the same kinds of persons who manage other business, political, and social affairs; that does nothing to close the credibility gap. Furthermore, the directors often are not trained welfare workers. In fact, some of the earlier public-relations rhetoric ostentatiously proclaimed that the direction of this *really* important project was deliberately to be withheld from those who had already failed in their welfare efforts. Such rhetoric was not likely

[22] Sar A. Levitan, *The Great Society's Poor Law: A New Approach to Poverty* (Baltimore: The Johns Hopkins Press, 1969), p. 121; statistical data, pp. 10, 120, 123.

to enlist the hearty cooperation of the professional social workers. In any case, funds allocated are but a small proportion of welfare expenditures which, say the social critics, have already proved to be grossly inadequate for the elimination of poverty. Supporters of the program therefore can charge hypocrisy in introducing a program fated to failure through non-support. If the CAP has not lived up to its press releases, there is at least no doubt that it has alleviated some poverty, and perhaps the dollars spent by it have been as well-spent as any other welfare dollars. A more definite judgment of success must await experience and the accumulation of reasonably hard data.

Education

In view of Americans' faith in the value of education as a cure for poverty it was entirely natural that it should figure prominently in the WOP. Two programs particularly were the focus of public attention: Head Start, which affected poor children at the beginning of the formal education process, and the Job Corps at the end of it. They were equally poles apart in popularity.

The Head Start program was based on the fact that poor children performed in school at a level far below the national average when they entered and slipped further behind as the years went by. The idea behind Head Start was to take pre-school children and give them food, medical care, and pre-school training that would help to make up their cultural lag upon entry into formal public schooling. Large number of non-professionals as well as professionals were used in the program. The sentimental appeal of children's programs helped to make Head Start the most popular of the War on Poverty programs despite its very doubtful success. Begun as a summer program, in the second year it was extended to a full-time pre-school program. Children exposed to a significant amount of Head Start training at first did more nearly approach the national average in performance, but follow-up studies showed that within a year or so the Head Start children were back to the level of other poor children. Training was not the sole purpose of Head Start. Improved nutrition and medical care presumably had some beneficial effect, however temporary. Nevertheless there was some disappointment over the comparatively short duration of the benefits. There was little surprise, however, since the results corresponded to common-sense expectations. The prevailing public attitude was that gains achieved by Head Start needed to be reinforced by general improvements in the total educational environment of the poor.

At the other end of the spectrum of popularity is the Job Corps, the vocational training program for teen-agers. Vocational training itself is the approach favored by Congress and business for alleviating poverty problems since it assures a supply of skilled labor that can be used immediately by the economy. Tax-consumers thereby not only enter the self-supporting labor force, but become taxpayers, thereby benefiting the community as well as themselves. Nevertheless the Job Corps was unpopular from the first. A major factor contributing to its unpopularity was the debt the concept owed to the Civilian Conservation Corps of New Deal days. Some of the first Job Corps centers were even located in conservation areas. The CCC had been one of the few New Deal programs of which little ill was said, but the 1960s were not New Deal days. The central purpose of the CCC had been conservation, and that of the Job Corps vocational training. Critics thought it made little sense to locate Job Corps training centers in conservation areas, and Job Corps trainees who were removed from urban environments and dispatched to uncongenial surroundings agreed with them. Urban centers were only a little more popular; residents were often apprehensive of the concentrations of poor youth, who were feared to be delinquents. There were enough delinquents among them to lend substance to the fears. At best, their life style as cultivated in the slums was revolting to the better-off residents of the communities in which most of the Job Corps centers were located. The centers for girls aroused some of the greatest hostility, particularly one located in the retirement haven of St. Petersburg, Florida. The elderly folk there had little sympathy with the disruption of their placid life-style by the vigorous and occasionally misbehaved young people. That center was eventually moved, the only one actually to be closed because of public opposition.

The essential question of course is, Does the Job Corps serve its purpose? The analysis of effectiveness is very complex and lends itself to interpretation made to fit the biases of individual critics and supporters. No really satisfactory data are at hand, but there are some fairly substantial indicators, principally the results of a Lou Harris poll of the Job Corps graduates of 1966 made during 1968. The short lapse of time between the graduation and the survey limited its usefulness. Briefly, the findings seem to be that many selectees do not report for training (often because of administrative shortfalls); some twenty to thirty percent of entrants drop out or are discharged before they have had a significant degree of training; those who graduate from training programs of up to six months' duration find jobs more readily than the drop-outs and receive higher pay, though the differential fades out

within eighteen months after graduation; and those who
are in training for six months or longer seem to show significant differentials over no-shows, drop-outs, and shorter-
period trainees. There is therefore some suggestion that
training periods of six months or more may be required to
yield statistically significant results. This finding is particularly important because although legislation permits
the enrollment of trainees for as long as two years, no program of longer than nine months is in effect, primarily
because of the drop-out problem.

To remain in the training program for extended
periods would seem to require character traits such as the
motivation to enter the middle-class life style, the ability
to recognize opportunities, the determination to profit by
them, and the persistence to see the program through —
a configuration of traits characteristic of middle-class
upward-strivers. Would persons with those traits have
escaped poverty anyway? Of course no answer can be
given, but it is difficult not to believe that at least some
proportion of marginal persons were salvaged by the Job
Corps program.

Salvaged, perhaps, but at what cost? Critics of the
program charged it with extravagance, some hostile estimates ranging as high as $30,000 per student.[23] The Job
Corps officials denied any such extravagance, but themselves allowed a credibility gap to appear. Cost accounting
is at best an art, not a science. Any administrator worth his
salt can within very wide limits make statistical conclusions support the views he holds. The estimate that appears most valid is that for fiscal year 1967: $7,357 for

[23] "Controversy over the Federal Job Corps," *Congressional
Digest* 47, p. 1.

conservation centers, $8,737 for men's urban centers, $9,602 for women's urban centers, and an overall average of $8,077.[24] Even that level of expense considerably exceeds the annual costs of education in our most expensive private colleges.

In response, supporters of the program contend that the critics do not take into account the fact that costs are bound to rise sharply as entrants are selected from progressively lower ranges of the aptitude curve. The Job Corps takes all comers and does its best to make something of all of the entrants. The supporters of the program therefore could point out that they were dealing with youths who suffered from years of cultural deprivation, and that it was simply not reasonable to expect them to conform in any short period of time to middle-class performance expectations. Supporters of the program include both classical liberals and welfarists, though for different reasons. Classical liberals support the vocational-training idea while having prudent regard for costs. Welfarists support the program on emotional grounds and are prone to profess a lordly disdain for pecuniary considerations where the cultivation of human values is concerned. Humane as that attitude may be, it affords no ground for reconciling the differences of opinion between classical liberal and humanitarian supporters of the Job Corps.

That is regrettable, for a rational argument can be

[24] Job Corps estimate cited in Levitan, p. 287. The differences in cost between men's and women's urban centers are due principally to the fact that somewhat more comfortable facilities were leased for housing the women. Former military barracks and similarly austere facilities were used for the men. There is of course no reason for Job Corps men to be housed more comfortably than our soldiers. The use of barracks, however, impelled the establishment of some centers in unfavorable locations.

made for rather high expenses for the salvaging of impoverished youth. To raise and condition a youth from a middle-class family over a period of some twenty-two years costs something on the order of $30,000. The situation does not excite public concern because most of the expenditure is borne by the family rather than society. Poor youths, however, suffer from cultural deprivation *principally* (the welfarist's unexamined assumption) because their families cannot spend similar amounts on them. Consequently, if the Job Corps' expenditures are viewed as remedial, intended to close the performance-expenditure gap with the middle-class youth, the figures are not unreasonable if it can be shown that the Job Corps really is salvaging a satisfactory proportion of the entrants.

All of that can be true and still leave unanswered the question: How many of the poor youth can be salvaged at acceptable cost? How far down on the ability curve is it worth while to go, before custodial care is cheaper than remedial training? It is obvious that the whole evaluation of the program is in such a nebulous state that no satisfactory answer can be rendered. Aptitude testing as yet cannot guarantee accurate prediction of performance. Above all, in education at all levels from pre-school nursery to post-doctoral training the name of the game is *motivation*. With enough motivation pedagogical technique becomes almost irrelevant; it is difficult to keep the student ignorant if you try. Without it, pedagogical technique is also irrelevant; he won't learn anything no matter how hard the teacher tries. Gifted teachers are infinitely imaginative in encouraging motivation, but even the most gifted cannot motivate everyone, and some persons seemingly cannot be motivated by anyone. Furthermore, it is statistically impossible for all teachers to be gifted. Most of life's activities have to be conducted by average people; consequently social institutions have to be designed so that average people can make them work. The conclusion is inescapable that for any program whatever there will be a residue of the mentally or physically impotent, and persons of unsuitable characters, whom no amount of training will salvage. If society is not to eliminate them it must have some other means of caring for them.

Conclusions

The treatment of poverty problems in America has followed traditional patterns considerably modified by local peculiarities. The basic conclusion is that in America as everywhere we have applied Nicholls' Principle. The means of support at first consisted of modifications of Elizabethan Poor Law and charitable practices with administration a local responsibility. The breakaway from those practices was very delayed in comparison with the European societies. The delay apparently was due to America's strong commitment to individualism reinforced by the strong commitment to the Puritan ethic. It is worth noting too that American prosperity reached full flower only at about the time when European economies had peaked out and were in trouble; there was little reason for pragmatists to adopt social practices from apparently-decadent societies.

The breakaway from Old Poor Law practices came only when American morale was shaken by the Great Depression. Even then the breakaway was incomplete; the practices instituted established a halfway station on the road to a social insurance state, with a few important New Poor Law features added. The only (nearly) complete coverage was afforded by pensions to the old. Each extension of the Social Security Act has had to be justified anew. The extension of medical care in particular occasioned a debate on principle insofar as Americans engage in such debates. It mobilized in opposition one of the most powerful pressure groups our political system affords. The defeat of that pressure group implied as nearly a commitment in principle to the extension of social welfare as Americans are likely to make.

The introduction of New Poor Law practices also was a halfway measure, amounting essentially to the provision of funds from the federal treasury for certain specified programs. Completeness of coverage of welfare needs was neither sought nor claimed. Insofar as both settlement and administration remained under state control, an important feature of the New Poor Law was not introduced. Consequently there can be considerable variation in welfare practices across the land. As to whether or not that is an evil is open to question. It facilitates the perpetuation of abuses stemming from local cultural patterns, as in the case of segregation in the South. By the later 1960s, however, the opinion seemed to be emerging that the South no longer could fulfill its role as the national whipping-boy; racial abuses elsewhere were no more attractive. The most serious consequence of local variation in welfare practices seemed to be the encouragement of the conversion of the urban centers outside of the South into holding camps for the impoverished.

The 1960s, our period of greatest national prosperity, saw also a renewed drive against poverty which was marked by some of the most impassioned and irresponsible rhetoric our political history reveals. Introduced by a president who in his own lifetime had only marginal political support, the War on Poverty suffered further by being surrounded by an aura of cynicism. It really had little new to offer aside from the questionable program of permitting a degree of participation in administration to the poor themselves. At best it could hardly have lived up to the public relations program that heralded its advent; but even making due allowance for Madison Avenue flatulence, the doubtful success of the program and the consequent disillusionment has been enough to give state altruism a bad name.

The costs of the welfare programs by 1967 had risen to massive proportions. In that year they exceeded $100 billion including education, or $65 billion without it. Total expenditures amounted to 13.1 percent of gross national product. No one therefore could claim that the poor were being neglected, either in absolute or relative terms. America, however, is the homeland of pragmatism. The question we ask ourselves is not, Are we spending a lot of money? but, Are we doing the job we should and could be doing? It is to that question that we must turn.

PART 3

POVERTY IN AMERICA: WHAT IS ITS FUTURE?

The writings on the subject of poverty in contemporary America in general reflect four points of view: those of the conventional socialists, the classical liberals, the traditional millenarians, and the cybernationists. We can conclude our discussion of poverty and its remedies with a review of those schools; examine their conclusions in the light of perspectives lent by our knowledge of poverty practices as they have evolved and been tested in the context of Western civilization; select the solution or combination of solutions that best seems to reflect the consensus of expert and popular opinion; analyze the assets and liabilities of the most plausible course of action; and attempt to predict the most likely course of events if it is adopted.

The Conventional Socialists: The Affluent Society

A professional economist of Keynesian views, John Kenneth Galbraith is best known for a number of books in which with a characteristic urbanity and wit he acquaints the diploma elite with the Keynesian interpretation of our economic environment. An adviser to government, a director of the wartime Office of Price Administration, and former ambassador to India, he has considerable experience in the management of public affairs. He is an advocate of the managed economy and favors equality in distribution of goods; he can therefore be considered a socialist within the definition of that word as used herein. He does not apply the word to himself.

The title of *The Affluent Society* is widely misunderstood. It is not a paean of praise for our economic achievements. Rather the author castigates the "conventional wisdom" of those who fail to comprehend that the millennium of plenty for all, merely dreamed of wistfully as recently as Keynes' day, has arrived, and that economic affairs in a society of plenty must be managed quite differently from those in a society of scarcity. In accordance with the conventional wisdom of the Keynesians he argues for compulsory redistribution of income by the government to promote the investment that it thinks best for the community, and particularly to promote expenditures on public services to which all would have equal access. He favors economic equality, although his chapter on the subject is couched in tones of resignation because for some unaccountable reason the agitation for equality has declined. He dismisses the question of poverty rather briefly, regarding the poor as remnants of the deprived who can be taken care of rather easily by a managed economy. He was charged by Michael Harrington with having underestimated the extent and depth of poverty; in the second edition of his book he denies the charge, but still does not attach as much importance to poverty as the millenarians.

Galbraith therefore believes that we now enjoy enough material prosperity to satisfy any reasonable community. Like most other commentators, he assumes this condition to be unique in history. There is no evidence that he has tested that assumption. We have already seen that, while not the rule, affluent societies are by no means uncommon. In fact, we are now able to define what is meant by an affluent society — which Galbraith does not do. An affluent society is one in which the members feel that they have achieved a comfortable ecological balance. A dynamic balance, one in which the society feels comfortable while continuing to adjust the ecological balance further to its satisfaction, is certainly conceivable. As a practical matter, the examples of affluent societies available to us are those in which material progress has ceased, or at least is advancing at an imperceptible rate. Galbraith's theory of the affluent society therefore leads to a presumption that what he is talking about is a society with an economy stagnating at a comfortable level. Keynesianism was developed in the first place as a corrective for an economy stagnating at a low level; it would not be remarkable if it were brought up to date as a formula for stagnation at a high level. If the economy has to stagnate at all, a high level is better than a low one; and if a community of stable size is living in material comfort, there is no need to define progress in material terms. This of course leaves unanswered a larger question: Can a stagnant economy remain affluent? Is not economic growth a condition of affluence? That question must be dealt with by economic theorists.

The Classical Liberals: Capitalism and Freedom

Opposed to the ideal of the managed economy is Milton I. Friedman of the University of Chicago, the most influential contemporary spokesman for classical liberalism. Friedman uses the word "liberal" in its original meaning, the doctrine that supports freedom as the organizing principle of society. He denies the right of any person or institution to intervene in the conduct of one's affairs beyond the bare minimum necessary to prevent infringement on the freedom of others and to protect the community from its enemies abroad.

The classical liberal simply denies the socialist assumption that individuals can manage an economy as effectively as the operation of a free market. Friedman even argues that government intervention in the Great Depression did more harm than good. The liberal also believes that personal freedom can best exist in a free-market environment in which no man is dependent for his welfare on any one person or institution; the free market, in providing the widest range of possibilities for earning one's living, affords the surest means of achieving independence from the control of others. The views of the socialists and of the classical liberals are irreconcilable. Persons hold one or the other opinion because of their outlook on life, not because of any conclusions that can be verified scientifically.

The classical liberal doctrine affords the maximum opportunity for making one's own way, but also imposes the maximum obligation to do so and minimum shelter for those who cannot or will not care for themselves. What is to be done about that latter group, the "sturdy beggars" of Elizabethan terminology? When Nicholls' Principle conflicts with the social injunction at least for self-support, it is Nicholls' Principle that governs. That creates a social neurosis; society is compelled by one ethical principle to do something that violates another. In the heyday of classical liberalism the solution was the attempt through the New Poor Law to compel men to discharge their social responsibilities, to compel them to be free. The experiment was a failure. It is simply a fact of life that there are always some who are not fitted for the struggle even for survival, let alone prosperity, in the competitive world of the free market.

Even in speculation the classical liberals have rarely advanced the idea of letting the socially-unfit sink if they cannot swim, and Friedman makes no such suggestion. Unlike Spencer, he shrinks from the Darwinian conclusion of his own arguments. His escape from the dilemma is to advocate a Guaranteed Annual Income for the socially dependent. He has proposed one of the more popular devices for administering it, the negative income tax. He also advocates public education by means of free-enterprise schools with tuition paid by government vouchers. Between the GAI and subsidized tuition Friedman advocates redistributive practices which would satisfy most socialists other than outright egalitarians.

The Millenarians: The Other America

The real heat of the debate over poverty was contributed by the outpourings of neo-millenarians such as Michael Harrington. His book is an impassioned cry of indignation that poverty is permitted to exist in the affluent society, in which, he believes, no possible justification for its perpetuation can be given. He demands an instant cure of poverty by any means available regardless of merely rational analysis. His position is simply that there is plenty of wealth in the community to provide everyone a "decent life" (a term which he does not define), and no merely conventional or rational considerations should be allowed to interfere with sharing of income. Like Galbraith, he postulates the obligation of society to redistribute wealth to the satisfaction of the constituency for which he speaks. While not explicitly demanding equality of sharing without regard to social contribution, fulfillment of the millenarian demands presumably would end in equalization.

Harrington, true to his millenarian orientation, puts forward no concrete programs of his own for implementation of increased sharing. His message is inspirational, not operational. His single significant foray into logical analysis is the attempt in an appendix to support his definition of the scope of poverty. His statistical homework has been done for him by others, particularly by Robert J. Lampman and Leon Keyserling. The conventional wisdom of the millenarians is rooted in currents of Christian thought at least 800 years old. Harrington, indeed, appeals to the charitable spirit in words worthy of Sir Charles Loch himself. That rings a curiously atavistic note to the button-down generation.

The Cybernationists: Free Men and Free Markets

The socialists, millenarians, and classical liberals add nothing new to the arguments over poverty as they have been conducted at least since the introduction of the money economy some 2,500 years ago. It is possible that a new school of thought, associated with the concept of "cybernation," does add something. Robert Theobald is the best-known spokesman of this school. A professional economist and a socialist whose philosophy is essentially the same as Galbraith's, he simply presses Galbraith's hypothesis of the affluent society a step further, arguing that with the advent of the computer a totally new factor has been introduced into production. He thinks we can expect a flood of production at the hands of a very small part of the population, the majority being idled by the most massive technological unemployment the Western industrial economy has ever seen. The potential glut of goods would realize the affluent society on a scale beyond the imaginings even of Galbraith, whom Theobald considers "surprisingly conservative." It behooves the community to prepare for the glut of goods and the attendant unemployment, and of course the glut should be translated into material plenty for all. Again he urges adoption of a Guaranteed Annual Income with a constitutional guarantee for its provision. He does not argue for immediate equality. He would accept as much as a three-to-one inequality at least in a transitional phase to ease the shock for the well-to-do middle class who are now established, but who will be put out of work by cybernation. Implicit is the assumption of eventual equalization. Theobald puts forward his thesis with a truly millenarian fire and would really belong to that group but for the fact that his arguments purportedly are based on scientific as well as millenarian grounds.

The validity of his arguments depends on one's interpretation of the significance of the advent of computers. Most of us today view them simply as machines like other machines which add to our productive capacity in much the same way that other machines do. In that view, the

advent of computers simply represents a further development of the industrial revolution that began some 250
years ago. If true, the changes resulting from the introduction of computers will be of the same kind and magnitude as changes resulting from other advances of technology. Theobald on the contrary maintains that the first
phase of the industrial revolution was marked by the introduction of power sources that replaced man's muscles. He
believes the computers with their associated control mech-
anisms to be analogous to man's brain and nervous system, and that the mechanization of thinking and controlling processes will superimpose upon the power revolution
a cybernation revolution of the same magnitude and
socially-revolutionary implications. By this means, says
Theobald, man will become free for the first time — free of
economic need. On that point Theobald uses the word
"freedom" in the conventional socialist sense, which is
antithetical to the way in which the classical liberal uses
it. The resulting semantic confusion seriously impedes
communication on a vital point.

Poverty: The Scope of the Problem

It is evident from the above presentations that these
writers have not been of much help in defining the scope
of the poverty problem. The concept of poverty is as elu-
sive as ever. The least common denominator of definition,
the bare material minimum of goods necessary for subsistence, is only marginally a part of the argument. Harrington, in fact, observes that "there is starvation in American society, but it is not a pervasive social problem as it is
in some of the newly independent nations."[1] Seligman

[1] Michael Harrington, *The Other America: Poverty in the
United States* (New York: The Macmillan Company, 1964), p. 177.

says that "no one asserted that starvation was rampant," [2] and later that "on the basis of minimum essential facilities, . . . only 5 percent of white families and 10 percent of Negro families can be said to have had poor housing in 1963." [3] In 1969 there was a flurry of interest in the problem of starvation, the millenarian assault being carried to that front as well, and a presidential commission was established to root out the pockets of starvation. The hunger-seekers found some, including appearance of nutritional diseases such as kwashiorkor (identified at the time with distress in Biafra) usually associated with the most desperately-deprived peoples. There was as yet no evidence to support the belief that an appreciable proportion of Americans suffered from hunger. President Richard M. Nixon, however, agreed that the existence of any hunger was intolerable and used the data for its existence as part of the rationale for the reform of welfare practices advanced by his administration.

The "Poverty Line"

In attempting to define poverty various statisticians relied upon the "poverty line" concept which has become conventional since Charles Booth's day. The best-known of such criteria was that established by the Council of Economic Advisers, which for 1962 fixed the line at $3,000 per year for families and $1,500 per year for unrelated individuals. By those criteria about 33.4 million persons, or about 18 percent, were poverty-stricken. Those criteria, however, were called into question for their statistical crudity. Mollie Orshansky in 1965 used a considerably

[2] Ben B. Seligman, *Permanent Poverty: An American Syndrome* (Chicago: Quadrangle Books, 1968), p. 17.

[3] Seligman, p. 26.

more refined analysis by factors of age, sex of head of family, and farm versus non-farm, and arrived at poverty lines for each based on an estimate of minimum food needs with a multiplier for other necessaries. Her conclusion also was that about 18 percent of the population lived in poverty, although not necessarily the same 18 percent.[4] It appears that if fixed criteria are used (adjusted for changes in the value of the dollar) the proportion of the poor is declining, but at a very slow rate. Leon Keyserling concluded that since 1947 the proportion of the poor had declined by about 1.9 percent per year, at which rate "it would take about another 45 years to liquidate family poverty in the United States. Such delay is unacceptable." [5] To whom it is unacceptable and why he did not say. It is typical of the poverty dispute to assert as facts what really are debatable matters, at least in the view of some.

Beyond that, the definition of poverty was expressed in nebulous terms. Harrington emphasized two aspects of poverty. "First, there are new definitions of what man can achieve, of what a human standard of life should be . . . in terms of the technically possible, we have higher aspirations. Those who suffer levels of life well below those that are possible, even though they live better than medieval knights or Asian peasants, are poor." Related to this technological advance is the social definition of poverty. "The American poor are not poor in Hong Kong or in the sixteenth century; they are poor here and now . . . they are dispossessed in terms of what the rest of the nation enjoys,

[4] Herman P. Miller, "Changes in the Numbers of the Poor," in Margaret S. Gordon, ed., *Poverty in America* (San Francisco: Chandler Publishing Company, 1965), pp. 82–87.

[5] Leon H. Keyserling, *Progress or Poverty: The US at the Crossroads* (Washington, D. C.: Conference on Economic Progress, 1964), p. 17.

in terms of what the society could provide if it had the will . . . if there is technological advance without social advance, there is, almost automatically, an increase in human misery, in impoverishment." [6] He introduces a new element in stressing the loss of hope, the futility of aspiration, as an essential component in the definition of poverty.[7] Seligman too emphasizes the importance of hope: "Perhaps the most important element in poverty," he says, "is psychological — what aspirations do poor people have, what hope is there for them to break out of the cycle of poverty? . . . Most of the evidence suggests there is little hope indeed without massive public programs to break that cycle." [8] Mollie Orshansky asserts that "accepted standards of consumption" should set the criteria,[9] but does not say how the community might arrive at a consensus as to those standards or to whom they must be acceptable.

The substance of these views is that the contemporary debate over poverty almost exclusively concerns relative and subjective rather than biological poverty. A rolling definition of "poverty" is used which is based on the untested assumption that the poor are entitled to be supported by the community at a level of consumption corresponding fairly closely to that of other segments. It appears to stake a claim to the right of all to consume equally, although none of the millenarians devote as much discussion to equality itself as Galbraith does. This definition of poverty by the comparative consumption test is reinforced by the emphasis on what might be called the right to equality in hope of breaking away from impoverished conditions.

[6] Harrington, p. 178.
[7] Harrington, p. 10.
[8] Seligman, p. 26.
[9] Quoted in Seligman, p. 28.

The poverty line therefore can be fixed anywhere between the bare material subsistence level and that of consumption equality for all, and the estimates of the number of the poor cover nearly all the ground between. Robert Lampman, a University of Michigan economist whose publication of statistical data on income distribution in 1959 opened that aspect of the debate, observed that the estimates of the proportion of the poor could "reasonably range" from 16 to 36 percent of the population. The lowest figure is fixed by Rose Friedman at about 4.5 million (about 2.2 percent) on a material subsistence definition. At the other extreme is Harrington's estimate that some 40 to 50 million Americans are poor; he is supported by Keyserling, who to the 18 percent of the "impoverished" adds also the 18 percent of the "deprived" to arrive at a total of about 36 percent (66 million) Americans who suffer from poverty or deprivation.[10]

Rose Friedman's proportion of 2.2 percent is much lower than most Americans would accept. A more general assumption is that at least the lowest 10 percent in the income distribution are in distressed circumstances. Similarly, Keyserling's estimate of 36 percent is certainly extravagant; it includes large numbers of persons who would be startled and amused to discover that they were deprived. "That is admittedly an arbitrary definition," one Census Bureau consultant observes, "and any definition so generalized commits the statistical sin of being too broad for its britches."[11]

[10] Keyserling, pp. 22–23; Harrington, p. 182.
[11] Ben J. Wattenberg with Richard M. Scammon, *This U.S.A.* (New York: Pocket Books, 1967), p. 154. (Scammon was Director of the Census, 1961–1965). On pp. 152–153 the authors flatly state that Keyserling is wrong, and explain why they say so. Herman P. Miller, also a Census Bureau consultant, attacks Keyserling's views

How then is the scope of poverty to be fixed? The
number perhaps most frequently mentioned is about 36
million Americans, or about 20 percent of the population.
That is not far from the proportion estimated by Charles
Booth and Seebohm Rowntree in their studies of London
and York eighty years ago, yet all concede that our poor
enjoy the use of far more material goods than the poor did
then. The estimate of 20 percent also appears occasionally
in historical literature on medieval and classical times,
although no one claims that any estimate for those times
can be supported by statistical evidence. The 20 percent
estimate, in fact, appears so frequently that we are justified in stating the following conclusions:

If a material-sufficiency or any other fixed criterion is
used, biological poverty is statistically infrequent in the
United States and is diminishing at a rate that will see its
disappearance in our time even if nothing specific is done
about it.

If a relative definition of poverty is used, it will be
with us as long as consumption is in any way unevenly
distributed; and social convention will tend to define the
poor as the bottom 20 percent of the consumers.

Some cautionary observations must be made on the
above statements.

First, with respect to statistical data. A well-known
book of the early 1950s was entitled *How To Lie With
Statistics*. It was required reading in many government
offices and should be included in the reading of every
informed person. If it is not available, the writings on
poverty will do very nicely for a substitute. There has
rarely been as informative an exercise in statistical sophis-

in detail in *Rich Man, Poor Man* (New York: Signet Books, 1965),
pp. 71–95.

try. In particular, however, we must recognize that a "statistically infrequent" proportion of Americans, say 2.2 percent, still represents 4.5 million distressed individuals and gives cause for embarrassment if not anger. A hungry individual takes no comfort in the realization that he is statistically infrequent, and the American (Puritan) ethic impels his relief. The significance of "statistical frequency" in this context is to indicate the existence of a social problem; but there is no reason to demand that a whole social order be upset or destroyed for the benefit of a small proportion.

Second, the above definition is cast in terms of consumption rather than income. Dollar income is the criterion conventionally used in all discussions of poverty. Only recently has it been pointed out that consumption levels can be considerably more favorable than raw income figures would suggest. The distinction is useful if only because of the considerable range of public services open to all, such as the use of highways. Another example is television entertainment: the poor rarely lack their television sets, the programs are financed by advertising, and if the poor spend less than the prosperous they can hardly be bearing a proportionate share of the expenses. The distinction has the more pertinence in that advocates of steeply-graduated income taxation often propose not so much the redistribution of cash as its expenditure on still more public services. Carried to a logical extreme, it would be easy to imagine the extension of public services to a degree which would make a modest cash income relatively immaterial.

Third, we must again note that medical care is being added to the necessaries of life and health and its expense is approaching that of the other necessaries.

And finally, if in no other way the millenarians have

served a useful purpose in re-emphasizing the role of hope in defining poverty. The myth of a poverty-free America could develop because it was true that able men could always make their way on the frontier. With the closing of the frontier came also the closing of that avenue of hope. The maintenance of realistic avenues for the improvement of one's material condition to the economic level accepted by the community as comfortable remains an essential component in the relief of poverty.

"Rights" to Welfare: What Are the Sanctions?

A peculiar feature of much of the agitation for extension of welfare is that it is couched in the form of demands, often "non-negotiable" ones. The basis in right for making those demands rests entirely on simple assertions made by those who present the demands. No one, however, can be bound by another's simple assertions. The community on which the demands are levied is entitled to know what broader basis for welfare rights may exist, for that as well as the scope of poverty determines the commitment imposed upon the economically-productive persons.

Broadly speaking, there are three sanctions for social action: divine decree, social contract, and natural law. Which of the three apply to welfare rights?

Divine decrees are notoriously difficult to interpret. The authority of the church fathers enjoins charity, but not the indiscriminate charity now demanded by welfare advocates. Further, some theologians tell us that God is dead. Dead or alive, in the twentieth century there are few persons attempting to influence public opinion on political matters who appeal to Him directly for injunctions to social action. This logically should undermine the position at least of the millenarians. Logic, however, has little to do with attitudes toward poverty, and attitudes once based upon religious convictions continue to govern much social action. The millenarians therefore benefit by the strength of religious tradition.

Social contract enjoins certain actions upon the community by consensus of its members. If consensus alone were to govern, the poor would be entitled to relief only if the community agreed that they were, and only to the level that the community accepted. Theoretically, the community could also agree *not* to support the poor. Societies sacrifice the interests of the poor, the infant, the rich, young men, Negroes, and any other categories of persons whose sacrifice the community believes will benefit the whole. Under the social contract, therefore, welfare rights exist only because the society agrees that they do, and only for so long as that agreement continues.

Natural law carries us to the twin roots of welfarism, Stoic beneficence and the liberalism expressed in Nicholls' Principle. What appear to be human universals must be accommodated, for they probably reflect instinctual drives which are violated only at the risk of considerable harm to the community. Natural law therefore enjoins relief, but only at the lesser-eligibility level embodied in Nicholls' Principle.

As to the basis for welfare "rights," therefore, it appears that God must be left out of account. The remaining sanctions consist of a combination of natural law and social contract. The conclusion is that (1) natural law enjoins welfare rights in accordance with Nicholls' Principle to the extent of supporting the life and health of all fully-participating members of society, and (2) beyond that, to the level of physical comfort which the community by social contract is willing to grant, and for which the reward to the economically productive sectors is the

psychic gratification afforded by the exercise of beneficence.

The reservation must be added that if the rosy predictions of the cybernationists are fulfilled, and ample
material means for all become available, the entire grounds
for welfarism would be changed. The fulfillment of their
predictions is certainly conceivable; nevertheless the real
world at the beginning of the seventies was one in which
there was still need for allocation of resources. Realistically, what was indicated was a reallocation of resources
more to the benefit of the poor within the framework of
the three social sanctions. It is within that framework of
thought that the cures for poverty must be sought.

The Cure for Poverty: Constitutional Reform

The cure for poverty theoretically could range from
the very easy to the impossible, depending on one's point
of view. If one were to take the material-sufficiency definition, we could achieve an instant cure by giving the poor
some stated sum of money which would cost no more than
our present welfare program. If one takes the relative
definition of poverty, obviously the problem is incurable
by any means short of equalization of consumption. If
there is no general agreement on the definition of poverty,
there will be no agreement on the most satisfactory solution and there can be no general satisfaction with it. Since
there is no sign of a general agreement on the definition of
poverty, we cannot expect the development of a solution
that all will accept as theoretically satisfactory.

That sounds like a grim conclusion, but in reality
social problems are rarely settled to the satisfaction of all.
A practical definition of a satisfactory solution is that those
affected by it, even though not completely satisfied, see

the attainment of more refined solutions as entailing an unacceptably high risk of encountering greater dissatisfactions. In the jargon of economics, a satisfactory solution is reached when the marginal utility of the alternatives is not apparent. Within the framework of such a pragmatic approach to the solution of the poverty problem the attainment of consensus appears to be rather easy.

The solutions put forward for the relief of poverty fall into five categories: full employment, extension of the social insurance state, adoption of the welfare-state principle, acceptance of socialism, and egalitarianism.

Full Employment

Employment for all is the solution sanctioned by tradition, social convention, and the Christian ethic. It satisfies a number of human drives and violates none. Work satisfies the social imperative that all who benefit from participation in a community are obligated to contribute to it. It satisfies man's creative instincts. It affords a sense of identity, in that men are known largely by what they do. Goods and services are made available through work. A main thrust of the anti-poverty drive as recently as the Kennedy-Johnson War on Poverty was simply to make work available to all and to make all capable of useful and well-paid work. Nineteenth-century socialist programs often demanded no more than that the government be the employer of last resort, and as recently as the demonstration in Resurrection City that was one of the two concrete proposals that the real poor could put forward.

Work as a panacea unfortunately suffers from some major defects. Not all persons can work; the impotent poor are excluded from this means of relief. Not all should work at paid employment; the benefits derived from the labor of working mothers are obtained at very doubtful social cost. More difficult yet is the matter of involuntary unemployment. It is always with us, and the efforts of the Kennedy-Johnson administrations to manipulate the economy so as to afford labor for all created serious problems while only alleviating unemployment. The manipulation created jobs which were left vacant because the unemployed could not provide the quality of labor needed to fill them; the compensatory training programs scarcely dented the ranks of the unemployed; and the excessive investment, reinforced by the partial war economy attendant upon the war in Vietnam, contributed to an inflation which eroded the position of the middle class. The disaffected poor may be dangerous; a disaffected middle class certainly is. Few economic misfortunes are as corrosive as inflation. A decade of assaults on poverty left the unemployment situation about where it was to begin with. Basically, the attempt to create jobs was a make-work program, and those never have been very successful. While the attempt to solve the problem of unemployment by those means seemed reasonable at the time, it proved no more successful than the workhouse programs of the Elizabethan Poor Law.

We may note in passing that the sixties also saw a renewal of feminist agitation, one goal of which was to compel the community to accept women on an equal basis with men in all high-status occupations. The pros and cons of the argument do not concern us here, but one obvious result of the attainment of the feminist goal would be a sharp increase in competition for jobs and presumably a corresponding accentuation of the unemployment problem.

Enemies of capitalism often argue that unemployment is inherent in the system; only adoption of another socio-economic system can do away with the curse. However, it is not true that unemployment is peculiar to capitalism. Agriculture nearly everywhere is marked by seasonal unemployment. Vagrancy and beggary are evidence of unemployment in all civilized communities at all times. The pre-industrial Poor Law income-supplement system and attempts to afford work through workhouses evidence the existence of the unemployed. The Soviet Union and her satellites claim to have no unemployment; but we include in our figures those who are changing jobs and other categories which are found everywhere, so that incongruity in the reporting of unemployment renders comparison inexact. The whole problem of defining unemployment, in fact, is subject to much the same difficulties as that of defining poverty itself. If unemployment is found under a variety of economic systems, we must not naively assume that a change to another economic system will necessarily produce favorable results.

Finally, we must bear in mind that, so far as the problem of curing poverty is concerned, work is not an end in itself, but a means to other ends. If the cybernationists are correct in predicting the end of work for industrial man, then we will indeed have to change our entire attitude toward employment as a means of relieving poverty.

Perhaps the most serious problem of unemployment arises from the rising level of mental competence required of labor. There has long been little need for sheer muscle-power. In the computer age it is easy to imagine the development of a situation in which the only labor required is of such a level that it can be performed only by a small part of the population, leaving the remainder no other occupation than that of socially-useless consumers.

No one can predict the consequences. Theobald assumes that man would then be free (by his definition of freedom) to cultivate "truly human" faculties, which in his opinion are the esthetic and altruistic ones. His views remind one of those of Victorian reformers who urged education for the masses so that they might have access to the Bible and Shakespeare. What the working class actually read was the indescribable penny press, which thrived on exploiting the vulgarisms of sex, crime, and jingoism. Some Victorians concluded that the masses needed to be kept poor, busy, and out of mischief. We are now contemptuous of that belief; but there is plenty of ground for skepticism regarding the belief that granting material plenty to all without imposing responsibility for social contributions automatically implies a surgence of estheticism and altruism. Brutality, callousness, and empty self-indulgence are also "truly human" qualities which could as easily predominate in an idle and useless citizenry. Since the increase in leisure is a fact of present-day life, we are going to be confronted with the problem — or opportunity — whether there is a change in the system or not.

The Social Insurance State

The spreading of risk through voluntary cooperation in insurance associations is universally hailed as an impeccably liberal solution to the problem of risk, and thus the introduction of government-controlled insurance corporations has been comparatively easy. However, democratic governments cannot resist the forces impelling them to bring wider categories of the poor within the scope of the acts, as with our foray into socialized medicine. While those efforts achieve some temporary and limited relief, social insurance is not very effective in reaching the hard-core poor. If it is operated on an actuarially-sound basis, it requires the payment of premiums by its potential beneficiaries. This assumes the beneficiaries to have disposable income; therefore the very poor can hardly participate in social insurance plans. If non-contributors are supported through the social insurance mechanism the effect is to disguise transfer payments. Even those who advocate the free use of transfer payments may well be reluctant to accept such evasions of reality, which contribute to a loss of confidence in the credibility of public institutions. But in any case, a true social insurance system has never been able to help the lower strata of the real poor. Its inadequacies will be even more apparent if the predictions of really massive technological unemployment are fulfilled.

The Welfare State

The next most radical measure is the adoption of the welfare-state principle. The welfare state may be defined as one which attempts to supply a minimum standard of living to all, usually a "reasonably comfortable" one by community standards. It does not enjoin equality in consumption, nor does it necessarily impose government control of production facilities, although some welfare states do own at least some of the major facilities. Since all societies, including our own, afford at least minimum material subsistence to all of their members, it follows that all societies to some extent are welfare societies. The principal arguments arise over the machinery of rendering support, the level afforded, and the rights of sturdy beggars to any support at all. The transition from a Poor Law or charity system to a welfare state may be fixed at the point at which (1) the sturdy beggars as well as the impotent poor are explicitly accorded the right to poor relief, and (2) the level of relief is fixed at the line that the community as a whole considers "reasonably comfortable." The welfare state can be implemented through a number of devices, of which the Guaranteed Annual Income is currently the one most frequently put forward in the United States.

The Socialist State

The welfare state is embraced within the concept of socialism as we defined it previously — by applying the test of the social control of distribution. A full-fledged socialist, however, demands social ownership at least of the major communications and production facilities, usually seeks to eliminate great income inequality, and would prefer to attain complete equalization of incomes. A welfare state with its economy managed on Keynesian principles, a steeply-graduated income tax, and with the wage-price controls that Galbraith would accept, would be a socialist state. As the social definition of a "comfortable" level of support for the poor rose, and as social control of the economy increased, the welfare state theoretically would evolve into a full-fledged socialist state. In regions such as Scandanavia, however, welfare states have been operated for as long as two generations at a stage of arrested evolution. There are powerful countervailing forces operating to check the drift from welfarism to socialism. Those include entrepreneurism, the human drive to profit by one's own labor, and selfishness.

The Egalitarian State

The egalitarians explicitly demand that all be granted an equal share in the consumption of goods without regard to social contribution. A difficulty here is that "equality" is as nebulous a term as any we have dealt with. The only true equality would be an equal sense of psychic gratification with one's total life condition. Psychologists can testify as to the difficulty of determining the level of satisfaction even of individuals, let alone in comparing two or more individuals. Realistically, therefore, when we talk of equality we can speak only of material equality. Even here, however, a level of goods that is an irreducible minimum for one person may represent for another an embarrassing glut of objects with which he would prefer not to be bothered. A person who most enjoys the outdoors may obtain full psychic gratification from occasional fishing trips. His neighbor may be enthusiastic about the study of foreign cultures. If the latter were bound to an income level that did not afford foreign travel and had no right to obtain further financing for himself, he would suffer the pains of true impoverishment. If the fisherman were afforded the higher level he would not derive much marginal gratification from the surplus; the money would be "wasted." A Trappist monk would be sorry for both. Where, then, is equality to be found?

Presumably nowhere short of satisfying every material desire, and at this time there is no reason to anticipate that for the predictable future. More realistically, assurance could be given of satisfying every material need. But does that leave us very far from the present state of affairs? If it is true, as the weight of statistical opinion holds, that material want is statistically rare and diminishing toward zero in our time, then the poverty arguments principally concern allocation of marginal gratifications. The questions raised involve happiness more than need. An egalitarian can at present demand only a mechanical leveling of consumption. Whether that would afford more happiness to the whole community is doubtful.

The first step toward the leveling of consumption would be the appropriation of the "excess" income of the rich and its diversion to public expenditures. This would mean the revival of liturgies. The transformation of liturgies from voluntary to forced donations was associated with economic decline and the introduction of totalitarian tyranny. The associations in the cases of ancient Greece and Rome therefore are not encouraging; but both societies collapsed for additional and perhaps more important reasons. We therefore are not justified in drawing any simplistic equation such as "liturgies equal collapse" and "liturgies equal tyranny"; but the parallels are suggestive enough to invite sober thought before egalitarian ideas are implemented.

Finally, the egalitarian state presupposes the highest degree of centralized control of the economy, a feature discussed in detail below.

The Unexplored Alternatives

It is notable that despite the considerable amount of attention given to poverty problems in the sixties there are a number of tested methods of relief that are rarely mentioned.

Charity, the principles of which really underlie most of the present agitation especially by millenarians, apparently has been abandoned as a primary reliance. It is true that in the past charity has always been replaced by some form of state relief, but it has served its purpose often enough and long enough to suggest that it deserves further consideration.

Self-help is one category of poor relief with a long record of success which has the decided advantage of freeing the poor from dependency. There are some important self-help movements in effect such as the Black Muslims and those inspired by Saul Alinsky, but on the whole the remaining poor are not organizing their own efforts. The Community Action Program is not an exception to that statement, because the CAP was not established by the poor but by legislative fiat. The reason for its limited success is apparent. Unlike the Chartist and early labor movements, the CAP was created by the well-to-do middle class to achieve goals that they thought best for the poor. The two classes cannot share the same outlook, and there is no reason to expect that they should. Like the proverbial charity workers in Georgian days whose charity consisted of exhortations to the poor to reconcile themselves to the place in life to which it had pleased God to assign them, it must be expected that middle-class welfare enthusiasts will seek for the poor something other than they would seek for themselves.

Precisely the same is true of agitation by millenarians to relieve the poor. After all, they are merely one of the categories of middle-class welfare enthusiasts. Their cultural separation from the poor was very evident at Resurrection City in the spring of 1968. Nearly all of the whites in the City were millenarians, and it was principally from them that the most radical calls for social change and even violent revolution came. With few exceptions the real poor did not want to change society; they wanted it preserved so that they might have a piece of the action. Most of the real poor were seriously disturbed at talk of revolution.

Why are the poor not mobilizing for self-help? Well, of course our story is not fully told. They may yet do so. But probably the explanation lies in the fact that the poor today represent a really hard-core element. It is possible to be poor in America today, but it isn't easy, except of course for the impotent. The remaining sturdy beggars are largely those who cannot or do not profit by the very extensive programs for bringing them into paid employment. It appears that persons incompetent to arrange for a reasonably comfortable standard of living in today's affluent society are also incompetent to manage the economic and political institutions through which they could obtain a larger share of the national wealth for themselves.

The development of political clout in order to influence the operation of the political system could be viewed as a form of self-help. The most primitive means of influencing the system is the riot, which is an excellent way of getting attention. There have been times when the riot was practically institutionalized as a means of communication between the lowest and highest orders of society.[12] The poor in America have not yet taken up the riot as a political tactic, though they have made some use of the peaceful demonstration. The National Welfare Rights Organization (NWRO) is strong in New York City and has affiliates in many other cities. As a self-help organization it is somewhat suspect, however, because it was established and is operated largely by middle-class altruists. If the NWRO remains dependent on them it will function only as long as their interest lasts. Movements such as the NWRO previously have not had much staying power. In the long run, it seems unlikely that the poor can depend on any political clout that is developed by others.

One of the major trends in the political history of Western civilization has been the diffusion of power to ever-lower orders of society: successively from the crown to the lords, the lower gentry, the townsmen, the tradesmen, skilled labor, and finally to semi-skilled and unskilled labor. In every case the lasting gains were those that were wrested by each class in hard struggle from the class

[12] E. J. Hobsbawm, *Primitive Rebels: Studies in Archaic Forms of Social Movement in the 19th and 20th Centuries* (New York: W. W. Norton & Company, 1965), p. 115.

immediately above it. It would follow from this sequence that the lasting benefit to the remaining poor would be the gains it can wring from the lower-middle class. In the struggle their allies come from a class at least one removed (for the greatest class hostility is found between adjacent classes). That would account for the fact that the self-appointed spokesmen for the poor are the well-to-do diploma elite. If the remaining poor cannot develop the clout they need to wrest improvements for themselves, they are condemned to rely upon the beneficence of the better-off. It makes little difference to the recipient whether the beneficence is exercised through private charitable institutions or public welfare ones, or for that matter by whom it is administered. A person dependent upon a welfare program administered by Michael Harrington would still be dependent, although perhaps physically more comfortable in his dependency than if administered by others.

In the foregoing, two matters have been ignored: the assumption that the system oppresses the poor, and the race question. As to oppression, a general observation can be made that anyone will be oppressed who allows himself to be. The classical liberal holds that true freedom can only be taken, never given. Socialists hold the contrary view. One's opinions on that score are based on belief, not on demonstrable fact.

"Oppression" presumably means that the poor are kept in poverty for the benefit of some exploiting group. The more radical of reformist and revolutionary literature suggests the existence of a more or less conscious conspiracy on the part of proprietors to maintain a pool of cheap labor that can be put to work in good times and retired to the welfare rolls in bad. By that interpretation the welfare expenditures constitute a public subsidy to proprietors, who purportedly are the only ones to benefit by "the regulation of the poor." [13]

It is true that all charity and welfare systems under-write the support of the marginally-employable persons who pass in and out of the labor force as the fluctuations of the economy require. This is an indispensable function of the welfare system, and it should be recognized and taken into account in developing welfare reforms. Fried-man advocates the GAI partly for that reason. There are some who can manipulate the system to their temporary advantage, but it cannot be shown that the system was deliberately designed to serve that purpose. The poor are generally regarded as a drag on the economy by proprie-tors as well as others.

If there is oppression, who profits by it? The answer to that question makes it clear that the poor today are in an unprecedented and very discouraging position. In America they are a minority of the population. If they are being exploited it is to the profit of a very large majority, not less than 60 percent and probably 80 percent. They

[13] Frances Fox Piven and Richard A. Cloward in *Regulating the Poor: The Functions of Public Welfare* (New York: Pantheon Books, 1971) conclude that the welfare system runs through repeti-tive cycles. Wide-spread poverty breeds unrest which is allayed by direct relief, the welfare rolls multiply (a "welfare explosion"), direct relief is replaced by work relief, and that in turn by "work-enforcing" reforms which drastically reduce the welfare rolls and drive the work-capable to take any employment, however ill-paid. Their introductory chapters review welfare practises since Tudor times, and make an interesting parallel with Loch's book and this one. Most of *Regulating the Poor* is devoted to detailed examina-tion of the work-enforcing system in the United States since the New Deal. Their model is a bit too neat to fit anything but recent American experience, but the description of the system for manag-ing the movement of the marginal labor force between the welfare rolls and low-paid employment is very thought-provoking.

are the victims of the possibility that the old aristocrat, Alexis de Tocqueville, cautioned us against more than a century ago: that adoption of the principle of the greatest good for the greatest number entails the risk that the greatest number might conclude that their greatest good is served at the expense of the lesser number. Correcting the abuses of a small exploiting minority historically has proved hard enough; what hope is there for correcting the abuses of a large exploiting majority? That would be a very discouraging question indeed if there were proof of the oppression hypothesis. Fortunately, there is no real proof. Of course plenty of individuals and institutions are unscrupulous enough to oppress when they can. In an anarchic economic system, however, it is usually the case that attempts at undue exploitation by one party harm others of equal force, so that countervailing powers check each other.

One area in which it appears that there is tacit agreement on the part of the majority to exploit a minority perhaps is race relations. The race question is relevant to this aspect of the problem since it appears perfectly possible to solve the problem of poverty for all others, but to leave some blacks still in distress. We need not elaborate further on that point because the solution of the poverty question for others implies also the means for solving it for blacks as well, if the will is there. The question of the will to deal rightly by them is by far our gravest social problem, but it is not the subject of our present discussion.

The Solution for Poverty: Advantages of the Guaranteed Annual Income

In studying the four principal schools of thought it is apparent that socialists, liberals, millenarians, and cybernationists are agreed on one conclusion: that the problem of poverty is best dealt with by the device of the Guaranteed Annual Income. That system also conforms well to the welfare state concept, which seems to be the most acceptable compromise between the social Darwinist world of classical liberalism and the egalitarian world of the socialist. Furthermore, it can be viewed as being merely one way of applying Nicholls' Principle, thus having sufficient sanction of tradition to satisfy conservatives.

There are many, perhaps most of those who have not examined the problem carefully, who are opposed to the GAI on grounds of "no work, no pay." It is always galling to support sturdy beggars. Nevertheless, societies always do support them by one device or another. Since that's the way it is, the next step is to determine the kind and cost of the commitment. The GAI, particularly when implemented through the administrative device of the negative income tax, affords a particularly easily-managed method of determining levels of cash support. The economy and efficiency of administration appeals to classical liberals.

The GAI affords the readiest device for adjusting the level of cash income to conform to whatever the community decides is a reasonably comfortable level of support to the poor.

If millenarians and egalitarians were ever able to induce the community to accept the principle of equality, its achievement could be attained by simply raising the level of GAI support to the egalitarian level.

If the cybernationists are correct and our problem will be to distribute a glut of goods, that too could automatically be accommodated by the GAI.

The GAI therefore affords a mechanism for basic support of the poor with minimum disruption to existing institutions and maximum flexibility for adaptation to the demands of social evolution.

Disadvantages of the GAI

It must be emphasized in the beginning that most of the disadvantages discussed below are not peculiar to the GAI; they are inherent in any mismanaged welfare program. They are discussed in this context only because it appears that some variant of the GAI affords the greatest likelihood of dealing successfully with our poverty problem.

Lack of Universality

The GAI would not answer to all poverty problems, in that money alone does not suffice to care for the blind, crippled, aged, orphaned, and like categories of the impotent poor. The GAI is neither more nor less well fitted to deal with them than other welfare systems, but at least no one should believe that it is a panacea.

Impersonality

For the millenarian, the impersonality entailed by the GAI must be a disadvantage. The only contact that the GAI gives the recipient with society is through the check deposited in his mailbox. The GAI, in fact, is antithetical to the classical tradition of Stoic and Christian charity. It is necessary to review the literature from all ages to appreciate how completely the concept of charity has dropped out of the discussions. Whatever one might have thought of the views of which Sir Charles Loch was the proponent, the charitable attitude was at least a humane one; the twentieth century has couched its arguments in the cold words of positivism. Only Harrington explicitly reintroduces the idea of charity when he pleads that

> . . . there should be a spirit, an elan, that communicates itself to the entire society.
>
> If the nation comes into the other America grudgingly, with the mentality of an administrator, and says, "All right, we'll help you people," then there will be gains, but they will be kept to a minimum; a dollar spent will return a dollar. But if there is an attitude that society is gaining by eradicating poverty, if there is a positive attempt to bring these millions of the poor to the point where they can make their contribution to the United States, that will make a huge difference. The spirit of a campaign against poverty does not cost a single cent. It is a matter of vision, of sensitivity.[14]

Centralization of Authority: The Managed Economy

The GAI entails centralization of welfare functions in the federal government, completing the evolution of social practices that began with the New Deal. The socialists, millenarians, and cybernationists assume that the GAI entails adoption of a managed economy, which they favor on doctrinaire grounds aside from the issue of poverty. Whether centralization is a disadvantage of course depends on one's point of view. The proposal further to centralize the management of the economy does, however, raise questions as to the competence of the authorities to manage it and the implications of the managed economy for the independence of the citizenry.

The classical liberal views the managed economy with suspicion because it revives the idea of rule by philosopher kings. That idea has always been popular with philosophers who would be kings, and with kings

[14] Harrington, pp. 167–168.

who would be philosophers, but not with anyone else. Actively to favor such centralized direction of the economy implies that one is prepared to repose confidence in the competence of technocrats to manage it. However, in rendering advice to government on any important real-life economic issue, such as control of the inflation of the sixties, economists of unimpeachable credentials and of equal reputation hold the most divergent and irreconcilable views as to the proper courses of action. The interpretation of economic events is obviously far from being scientific enough to afford the reliability in prediction needed for a managed economy. Furthermore, the managers of the economy are always under pressure to take economic actions against the advice of economists for political reasons. The imposition of a social security "contribution" on Roosevelt's insistence, discussed above, is an example. It follows that every managed economy will necessarily be mismanaged to some degree, and historical evidence indicates that the degree often will be large. Decry it as they will, the technocrats must accept that as a fact of political life. In short, enthusiasts for the managed economy simply offer what cannot be delivered.

Proposals for the managed economy also raise the question of the responsiveness of the managers. They would be bureaucrats, who are living, breathing, walking, talking, fallible human beings. In the organismic view of the world as seen by the socialist there is rarely any recognition of the consequences of that fact. We already have plenty of experience with the human being as bureaucrat. J. S. Schumpeter long ago pointed out that he was inheriting the earth, and Galbraith himself emphasizes that the great industrial enterprises today are managed by bureaucrats rather than entrepreneurs. It is usually mere personal accident that determines whether any particular individual becomes a bureaucrat for General Motors or for the Department of Labor. In the sixties there was considerable dissatisfaction in all quarters with the mismanagement of social affairs, often arising from the inertia and impersonality of governing institutions. There is no reason whatever to believe that the quality of management will improve in the future; on the contrary, as institutions become even larger and more monolithic, their inertia will become even more massive. The failure to recognize this is particularly inexplicable in Galbraith's case, since he has experience in government and has supplied a conventional denunciation of the State Department bureaucracy.

How then can Friedman favor the GAI? Partly because on that point he abandons theory, and partly on the lesser evil principle. He affords no theoretical justification for support of the poor. He simply accepts Nicholls' Principle as a fact of life, and seeks the most effective and economical means of fulfilling it. That necessarily entails a degree of management of the economy. All economies are managed to some extent anyway. All sovereign governments manage the money supply and operate at public expense all essential services that do not return a profit. Friedman recognizes those realities, but insists that they should not be used as justification for making an undesirable situation worse by extending social management beyond the bare minimum. While adoption of the GAI implies some management of the economy, he believes that its administration could be arranged so as to involve less management than we now have. His advocacy of the GAI therefore falls within the scope of adaptation of classical liberal theory to reality.

Centralization of Authority: The Threat to Freedom

It would almost not be too much to say that this is the most important factor in the debate over GAI. The advocates of the managed economy and the classical liberals hold antithetical views on this point. The socialists and millenarians maintain that by affording everyone a comfortable income our citizens will be freed of responsibility for their material welfare, and therefore be free to turn their attention to other and presumably more gratifying pursuits. This is an ancient theme in the socialist and millenarian traditions. In recent American political history it has been referred to as "economic democracy." It is asserted that one man who is paid a living wage by another is at his mercy and that to afford all a living income frees one from dependency upon proprietors.

The classical liberal rebuttal is that obviously the dependency is transferred to the central government; therefore the managed economy holds its greatest dangers from removing options as to sources of income. If a man working for General Motors finds his conditions of employment disagreeable, he can find more congenial employers. He might be inconvenienced by loss of income, in having to move his home, and so on. But the classical liberal does not feel impelled to protect individuals against all the vicissitudes of life, only against those that threaten life and health. If one's basic living income, or worse yet in the egalitarian state one's whole income, could come from only one source, the individual would be totally dependent upon that source with no recourse elsewhere. The consequences of defiance of that source are so disastrous that only a statistically-insignificant number of extraordinary individuals will defy a regime with such powers. The fate of Boris Pasternak and a number of other dissidents in the Soviet Union demonstrates that rather simple fact of life.

American dissidents certainly can get into serious trouble by defiance of authority, as was demonstrated during the period of McCarthyism. As Friedman points out, however, the persons who lost their positions or were blacklisted were able to re-establish themselves precisely because a free-market economy affords a wide range of choices of employers and of self-employment. The victims of McCarthyism of course paid a penalty for their convictions, but the classical liberal believes that no one need respect convictions for which their holders are not willing to pay a price. The fact that the price in a free-market economy is acceptable was evidenced by the flourishing of dissidence in the sixties. The very numerous and very provocative dissidents obviously entertained no very serious fears for their personal well-being.

It is really unaccountable that the socialists and millenarians do not take into account the possibilities for tyranny inherent in the managed-economy variant of the GAI. Theobald does recognize the potentialities, and therefore in his version of the GAI proposal he alleges that the GAI must be an *"absolute constitutional right"* (his emphasis), else "the most extreme form of tyranny imaginable" will ensue.[15] But would a constitutional guarantee be effective? It was the social reformer Frances Perkins who said to Justice Stone that "your Court tells us what the Constitution permits." It was the Supreme Court which in 1896 approved segregated facilities for Negroes, and in 1954 enjoined the integration of public facilities. Was Mr. Dooley unduly cynical or merely realistic when he averred that "th' supreme court follows th' iliction returns"? The very term "activist court" suggests that its function partly is to find constitutional grounds

[15] Theobald, p. 119.

for justifying measures that the community desires. To the minds of many persons there is already disturbing evidence of the lack of responsiveness of central authority. The sixties was the decade in which the actions of four successive presidents carried the country into its third greatest war (in casualties) without fulfilling the constitutional requirement for a congressional declaration of war; no recourse to the Supreme Court appeared feasible. The high level of dissidence that marked the decade was attributed by many observers to the already-existing lack of responsiveness of public institutions to public demands. How Theobald, Galbraith, and Harrington can justify a further extension of the already awesome powers of central government is incomprehensible. They need to explain themselves.

Furthermore, there is concrete evidence of the weakness of reliance on constitutionalism stemming from court tests of the Social Security Act. Roosevelt specifically required that OASI be couched in the form of an annuity system comparable with those of the private insurance companies. That implied a contract to the effect that those who made contributions were entitled by right to a return. Yet in 1960 the Supreme Court denied to one Ephram Nestor the right to collect benefits under OASI. Nestor was a native of Bulgaria resident in the United States since 1913 who had paid Social Security taxes since 1936. From 1933 to 1939 he had been a member of the Communist Party of the United States; at that time no legislation making such membership illegal was in effect. In 1954 Congress provided that a person deported because of past Communist membership should be cut off from Social Security benefits. In 1955 Nestor began drawing benefits. In 1956 he was deported and his OASI benefits terminated. He sued to recover on grounds that his property rights were being violated and that he was being punished for Communist Party membership under *ex post facto* legislation. On the first point, the U. S. Attorney's brief denied that "contributors" to Social Security have property rights therein. "Social Security," said the brief,

> must be viewed as a welfare instrument to which legal concepts of "insurance," "property," "vested rights," "annuities," etc., can be applied only at the risk of serious distortion of language . . . monthly benefit payments are voluntary payments to the recipient, property acquired by gift. . . . The benefits conferred may be redistributed or withdrawn at any time in the discretion of Congress.[16]

The Court concurred with this view, holding that the right of a Social Security "contributor" could not be "soundly analogized to that of a holder of an annuity"; thus Nestor was denied payments under OASI that a commercial insurance company would have had to pay. The OASI "contribution" was a bad bargain for him.

Furthermore, in denying Nestor the OASI benefits the Court added an argument of expediency, holding that

> To engraft upon the Social Security System a concept of "accrued property rights" would deprive it of the flexibility and boldness of adjustment to ever-changing conditions which it demands and which Congress probably had in mind when it expressly reserved the right to alter, amend or repeal any provision of the Act.[17]

In this case the "flexibility and boldness of adjustment" was demonstrated by imposing retroactively a political qualification for the receipt of benefits. To paraphrase

[16] *Flemming v. Nestor,* 363 U. S. 603. Quoted in Charles Stevenson, "How Secure is Your Social Security?" *Reader's Digest* (October 1967), p. 77.

[17] *Flemming v. Nestor,* 363 U. S. 610–611.

poor Roosevelt, "even with those taxes in there, some damn politicians *had* scrapped his social security program" as far as Nestor was concerned. Again, the privileged position of a government in this respect is a consequence of the fact that a sovereign government cannot be held legally accountable as can a private corporation. That does not mean that a constitutional guarantee is nothing, but it decidedly does mean that it is not everything.

Further with respect to the constitutional guarantee, it might be possible to assure a more satisfactory sharing of the production that does occur, but no constitution can guarantee an adequate level of production. The constitutional guarantee is based on the assumption that in a managed economy there will be no lack of goods, that is, there will be no economic disasters. Serious and prolonged economic disasters, however, result from irrational human behavior as much as anything else. Consider, for example, the Tulip Craze in Holland in the 1630s when speculation on the market for tulip bulbs bid the price up to several times their normal value. A severe depression followed the inevitable collapse. Now, the tulip is as innocent a flower as ever graced God's footstool. A creature that can build an economic catastrophe upon its roots is capable of anything.

Lack of Work Incentives

Again, one must review the whole literature on the subject to obtain a full impression of the curious world in which the socialists and millenarians dwell. It is a world in which no individual actually *does* anything. Economic events simply happen; no one makes them happen. Indeed, those socialists who are also cybernationists view work almost as an anti-social neurosis for which an acceptable sublimation must be found. Either the question of incentive is ignored, or it is denied that money need be used as an incentive.

As to the assumption that there will be no work to be done, it is hard to see how even the most devoted cyber-nationist can believe that that particular millennium will be achieved in the foreseeable future. They ignore the fact that a computer is stupid, or perhaps it would be more precise to say that a computer is like a small child in that it is dreadfully literal. It will do just exactly what it is told to do, neither more nor less. The art of talking to computers, which may be likened to cultivating the art of baby-talk, is a flourishing trade-craft and it is demanding much more labor every day, not less. We can well envision the day when "labor" might be defined as those who deal with computers; but at least that much labor must always be afforded, and it can be very nerve-wracking, tedious labor.

Also, it remains to be seen whether massive techno-logical unemployment really will occur. In 1967 Theobald predicted that by 1970 computer power would have in-creased 140,000 times over 1960 and implied that its effects on employment would be evident.[18] When that time had

[18] Theobald in Paul Jacobs et al., *Dialogue on Poverty* (In-dianapolis and New York: Bobbs-Merrill, 1967), pp. 110–111. George Terborgh in *The Automation Hysteria: An Appraisal of the Alarmist View of the Technological Revolution* (New York: W. W. Norton & Company, Inc., 1966), p. 95, concludes that "the alarm-ists . . . do not understand the process by which improvements in the technology of production have generated new jobs and expanded production heretofore . . . the adverse employment effects of auto-mation have been blown up out of all relation to reality." At the beginning of the seventies there was increased unemployment in connection with the attempt by the Nixon administration to check inflation, but it was of the scope to be expected from the conven-tional management of the economy.

elapsed, no revolutionary effect was apparent; rather the trend of events demonstrated the evolutionary hypothesis. In the nineteenth century the introduction of steam and the ensuing shift to manufacture was attended by a massive movement from farm to factory and a reduction of the need for farm labor to less than ten percent of the work force. By the 1960s a similar shift from the factory into service occupations was apparent; already the proportion of labor involved in production and agriculture together was less than half of the labor force. Man's appetite for food is limited and there is no reason why his appetite for other commodities should not also be limited. Consumerism accompanied the industrial revolution, and we may well join much of mankind in recognizing limits to its demands. There may also be a limit to his appetite for services; but no such limit is in view, and the present trends in labor-force dynamics suggest that it will absorb all the labor that will be available for the foreseeable future. Due to man's rolling definition of "needs," the need for services will be felt as acutely as once the need for bread and now the need for goods is felt.

Nor is there an immediate prospect that the progress of technology will do away with all of the hard, dirty, dangerous, menial, and difficult tasks that must somehow be performed in any society. In order to get them done there are only the two means available: the whip of need and the carrot of reward. Which do we choose? We presently use a blend of both: the whip of need to obtain garbage-collectors, the bait of reward for oil-well drillers. If our garbage collectors have an adequate living income, will they still collect garbage? We cannot simply assume that they will.

Socialists and millenarians argue that no one should be compelled to collect garbage anyway; that economic compulsion is no more attractive than police compulsion, and no more justifiable. That is a delusion entertained only by those who have known no police compulsion. Our urban centers contain many refugees from fascist and communist totalitarianisms who gladly accept any economic terms if only they can escape the rigors of the police state. Even the poorest of our employed have open to them far more choices than any other social system affords, grim as some of the choices may appear to unworldly Americans. The unemployed, of course, are another matter, and as we have already emphasized that problem is the rock on which the classical liberal philosophy threatens to founder.

Are incentives other than money effective in obtaining the necessary work? That is a question on which we really have no conclusive evidence. In smaller primitive societies other incentives have considerable effect, but they stem largely from the intimate personal relationships that are not available to any larger society. Anarchists and most socialists believe that it would be possible to obtain social services by mobilizing man's altruistic sentiments. In effect, that would mean rewarding work in prestige rather than in goods. That's something to think about. A large part of our present public-service activity is so motivated. Indeed, a Rockefeller or a Ford has little choice if he is to seek meaningful personal goals. Soldiers, police, teachers, ministers, and other public servants are partially so rewarded in compensation for pay scales that are somewhat unattractive in comparison with the qualifications required and the services rendered. In their better days the liturgies also were rewarded by prestige. With the possible exception of the priesthood, however, no extensive social service has ever depended entirely on that incentive for its production. Even the priesthood is questionable, since superstitious motivations play an important part; and also the church by its control of wealth affords very substantial economic incentives.

The Soviet Union has been attempting to create a New Soviet Man who would render services because of altruistic motives rather than from economic necessity or greed. As a practical matter, all existing socialist states use material incentives as well. The consumption differential in the Soviet Union between the working class and its favored artists and officials is as great as in our community. The Soviets do not deny this, and attribute the state of affairs to the imperfections of a system still in transition. The Soviet Union has also had to rely on generous application of the whip of the police state to obtain much of its social service. Whether police-state compulsion is necessary for operation of all socialist systems is a question that we will not try to resolve here.

There is one additional non-material incentive of significance: the striving for power. The few who do work in a highly technological society literally have their hands on the levers of power. In any managed economy, the philosopher kings who manage it would exercise tremendous power. The drive to obtain power is one of the motivations for certain persons to accumulate goods far beyond the capacity of any human being to enjoy them. In such cases it makes little difference where the title to property lies. It may be vested privately, in a church, or in the state; so long as the power-seeker can control it he has attained his objective. The managed economy sought by most GAI advocates affords unparalleled opportunity to obtain power together with social sanction for its exercise.

The classical liberal insists that such concentration of power is inherently dangerous and therefore unacceptable, and must be avoided at all costs in favor of diffusion of economic power among as many power centers as possible. Oligopoly is preferable to monopoly, and economic anarchy is best of all. Where monopoly must exist, it must be as limited as possible and the inherent dangers of the concentration of power must be recognized and guarded against as much as possible.

How then can Friedman favor the GAI? Simply by presenting the above case; by arranging the financing of the GAI so that its administration will be as automatic and impersonal as possible; and most importantly, by using the GAI to remove the rationalizations for most of the management of the economy that presently exists. By supporting impoverished farmers, for example, the monstrous network of controls over agriculture can be removed, resulting in a net gain to the community. It is not that the GAI would not require some management of the economy, but that its introduction could allow the dismantling of much of the existing machinery of centralized management. The degree of management envisioned by Galbraith, at least in the introductory stages, appears not to be much different from Friedman's; but what for Friedman is the outer permissible limit of management is for Galbraith merely a starting-point.

Distortion of the Wage Structure

This is a question on which there has been little discussion except from the one major opponent of the GAI, George Meany, president of the AFL-CIO.

It would appear paradoxical that the objection should come from the leader of what passes for the working class in America. That fact, however, should be coupled with the fact that advocates of the GAI include some of the well-regarded leaders of industry such as Dr. Edwin C. Land of Polaroid Land Corporation, one of the most successful entrepreneurs of our day, and Arjay Miller of the Ford Motor Company. On this point, as on many others having to do with wages, labor and some capitalists are opposed. Land and Miller and their kind may well be motivated by altruism; but we are justified in seeking self-interest as well, and self-interest is quite apparent to those familiar with the Speenhamland system. Under any wage-supplement system employers need not pay a full living wage, but only the difference between a living income and whatever supplement society is willing to provide. The effect of a supposed "supplement" therefore is to lower wages, and the supplement becomes an indirect subsidy to industry paid by the taxpayers. Industrialists therefore can favor the GAI, while Meany fears that it will depress the wages of labor.

Our economic system is considerably more complex than that of 18th-century England, and that fact might easily be disguised. The Speenhamland system appeared in the form of supplement to inadequate wages; the GAI would afford a floor to income, and in order to obtain workers industry would have to supplement the GAI with a substantial differential, thus raising the dollar cost of labor. The effects of that system are still the subject of speculation by professional economists. Three effects may tentatively be suggested: difficulty of maintaining wage incentive, inflation, and tax rebellion.

Socialists and millenarians ignore the problem of wage incentive. Friedman thinks that wage incentive can be maintained under a sliding-scale GAI. Other economists are not so sure. All compromises are more or less unsatisfactory, but all revolve around the idea of a sliding-scale GAI that would allow the laborer to work while retaining part of his GAI until his income reached rather generous levels. That system provides for as much income inequality as now exists and implies that the GAI would be low enough to afford incentive even for unpleasant work. It is difficult to imagine a millenarian who would be satisfied with that condition. As a technical problem, economists can project the probable costs of several models of the GAI-wage incentive system, most of which are financially acceptable.

A second outcome might be an inflation which would leave the poor about in their present relative position. If the GAI were funded with money from the programs that it replaced, that effect might be avoided. The GAI level would have to be very modest. It is also true that the proportion of GNP devoted to welfare is rising anyway, and while there is also an inflation, the inflation is due to other more important and more complex causes. We may therefore set aside the possibility of inflation unless it appears to assume greater significance in the future, but it should not be forgotten.

Far more important is the possibility that the GAI would afford a subsidy to industry, but disguised in the form of higher taxes for the workingman rather than a lowering of his wage level. The GAI would have to be paid for somehow. Socialists and millenarians assume that payment would be afforded by redistribution of income through the graduated income tax. One of the few things on which economists are agreed, however, is that the total tax system, including local and state property and excise taxes, is not redistributive. A redistributive system is certainly conceivable, but our fifty years' experience with the income tax is not encouraging. It is much more probable that the GAI funds would be contributed by the majority of middle-income taxpayers who supply most revenues now, so that the reduction of their income by taxation would be tantamount to the lowering of wages associated with the Speenhamland system.

Encouragement of Elitism

A by-product of a GAI tax structure would be an automatic control over the level of GAI afforded. A dynamic balance would be struck between the demand of the poor and the consent of the taxpayers. The control would be automatic as long as the democratic political system prevails. There is little reason to believe that the community would consent to support of the poor above the lesser-eligibility level, let alone at that of equality. Consequently, while a GAI would lift the poor out of biological poverty, in a democratic political system it does not seem likely that the taxpayers would consent to elimination of relative poverty. Voluntary leveling of consumption could be expected only if the rosiest predictions of the cyber-nationists were fulfilled.

Those inclined to do so will charge the lower middle class with selfishness, but charges of selfishness will not produce money for the GAI. That, as always, can be obtained only by force or persuasion. Democracy is based on persuasion. If it fails to produce what the millenarians consider "what a human standard of life should be," if society continues to "suffer levels of life well below those that are possible," then the socialists and millenarians will have but two recourses: to compromise their goals, or to abandon democracy. It is significant that the democratic principle is already under attack by certain of the most radical welfarists — although not by anyone mentioned in this book.

An attack on the democratic principle therefore can stem from the elitist attitude of some socialists and millenarians. They not only believe that they know what is best for man — a delusion shared by most of us — but are under compulsion to see to it that it is done, if necessary by themselves and by force. Those are the would-be philosopher kings. Carried somewhat toward the extreme and placed in an inflammatory situation, they can cultivate revolutionary elitism: the determination to do that which the intellectual believes is best for the society whether the society wants it or not. The GAI may be acceptable, but beware of the socialist or millenarian who is dissatisfied with the voluntary level of support accorded. He might well fancy himself a philosopher king.

The GAI: Pro and Con

Lack of universality, impersonality, centralization of authority, possible compromise of freedom, lack of work incentive, distortion of the wage structure, encouragement of elitism — that is an impressive roster of disadvantages. How is it possible to advocate a program that suffers from so many faults?

To repeat, those disadvantages are not particularly inherent in the GAI, but are equally true of all welfare systems, including our present one. Any welfare system, particularly as it applies to sturdy beggars, is a more or less unsatisfactory compromise between the social injunction that all should be useful and Nicholls' Principle requiring the support even of the socially useless. It is never possible to resolve such social conflicts perfectly, but only to the working satisfaction of most of those involved. The GAI would probably do that; in fact, it appears possible to arrange the GAI so that it has a simplicity, flexibility, and comprehensiveness unmatched since the early days of Queen Elizabeth's Poor Law. It is easy to understand its attractiveness to holders of such widely-differing views as Friedman and Theobald.

The Family Assistance Program

In August of 1969 President Nixon formally introduced a program for a comprehensive reform of the national welfare system. The principal feature is the Family Assistance Program (FAP), which is intended to afford a minimum income to each impoverished family even though the father is present in the household. Encouragement to self-reliance is afforded by the condition that the head of household enter training programs and accept work. Grants would begin at $1,600 per year for families with an income of less than $1,000 per year. Wage incentive supposedly would be maintained by reducing the grants on a sliding scale so that some payments would be continued until the family income reached the level of $4,000 per year. The aged, blind, and disabled would unconditionally receive a federally-guaranteed minimum income.[19]

The debt owed by those proposals to the GAI concept is obvious, although Nixon denies that the FAP is actually a GAI.[20] In his view, there are two significant differences. First, able-bodied persons, single or married, without dependents, would not be eligible for FAP. Second, fathers who could work but won't would not be eligible for benefits, although their dependent wives and children would be. He does not explain how relief to the dependents would be dissociated from relief to the father as long as the father is resident with the family.

[19] Richard M. Nixon, *Setting the Course: the First Year. Major Policy Statements by President Richard Nixon.* Commentaries by Richard Wilson (New York: Funk & Wagnalls, 1970), p. 59.

[20] Nixon, p. 53.

It is traditional to introduce reforms first on behalf of women and children, the dependents who are entitled to community support everywhere. It is then never possible to refrain from extending the system to the remaining dependents as well, including sturdy beggars. To repeat, under Nicholls' Principle *all* citizens receive minimum community support, if not under one program, then under another. It is difficult to believe that administrations less conservative than Nixon's would refrain from extending the FAP to the two excluded areas, thus transitioning into a full-fledged GAI, with all of the advantages and liabilities entailed. It is on that basis that we may best evaluate the worth of Nixon's proposals and conclude that, like other variants of the GAI, they afford the most practical means of reforming the welfare system.

Conclusions

Our society, like all others, will fulfill Nicholls' Principle. The most frequent suggestion as to the means of doing so is the GAI, whether by that name or another. Its comprehensiveness, flexibility, ease and economy of administration, and the readiness with which the charge on the community can be determined recommend it highly. The GAI's liabilities, while serious, are not peculiar to it. In some matters, as in the case of loss of work incentive, the liabilities may even be lessened because abuse is more easily perceptible and the extent of abuse more easily determined than with other systems. Its adoption would facilitate the elimination of some special privileges granted at public expense, such as protective tariff legislation, agricultural price support programs rationalized as poor-relief programs, and government relief of distressed industries.

The categories of the impotent poor whose poverty can be relieved with money will benefit adequately by the GAI. The record suggests that they will be given a level of support adequate not only to relieve destitution but afford a modest degree of luxury. Biological poverty can easily be eliminated by the GAI, although the evidence indicates that biological poverty will disappear in our time anyway whether any specific measures are taken or not. Reservation: "biological" poverty too is subject to social definition. It would be entirely possible continually to raise the standard so that it is never relieved. By nine-teenth-century standards biological poverty is infrequent today.

It follows that perhaps even biological poverty, and certainly relative and subjective poverty, will never be cured by the GAI or any other system as long as consumption is unevenly distributed. Introduction of the GAI there-fore will have only a temporary effect on the subjective mental states of the poor and their spokesmen. Mille-narians and egalitarians will continue to be as alienated and angry as ever. They will continue to demand equaliza-tion of consumption either explicitly or implicity by ad-vancing programs that have their natural conclusion in equalization.

The quarrel with advocates of extended welfare, as always, will turn upon the question of the able-bodied poor. The man who works and is taxed of part of his earn-ings to support the poor will always resent the impositions of those who are as mentally and physically able as him-self. There is no reason whatever to suppose that the com-munity will voluntarily consent to the support of the able-bodied at any but a lesser-eligibility level. It is impractical to afford different support to the able-bodied men and other categories of the poor such as their wives and chil-

dren — at least, not without breaking up their families.
Our present welfare system does that, and that is considered one of its major defects. The fulfillment of
Nicholls' Principle therefore in the case of the able-
bodied poor results in *de facto* application of the lesser-
eligibility principle not only in their cases, but in that of
their dependents, so far as cash grants are concerned. The
lesser-eligibility rule need not be applied in the case of
public services such as education.

Socialists and egalitarians will continue to demand a
change in the social system which would eliminate the
lesser-eligibility principle. The system is changing anyway, and very considerably to the advantage of the lower-
middle class of employed workmen. Furthermore, with the
growth in the proportion of the national economy devoted
to services there is a possibility of a renewed widening of
the scope of opportunity for the expansion of the small-
business category of independent proprietors. Therefore a
vast majority of Americans — at least sixty percent by any
estimate, and probably closer to eighty percent — have a
vested interest in the perpetuation of the present course of
social evolution. Agitation for egalitarianism therefore is
having no perceptible effect on the community.

Frustrated in his efforts to accomplish a social revolution by persuasion, the intellectual easily turns to revolutionary elitism and the attempt to change by force. Such a
trend is evident today, but so far only on the part of a
numerically-insignificant lunatic fringe. They have no
political power and no influence other than that arising
from the shock value of their extremism. The single significant exception to the statement arises from the race question. It is conceivable that legitimate racial grievances
could precipitate social unrest which revolutionary elitists
could capture and divert to their ends. The possibility is

far more remote in America today than in any community in which any such course of events has taken place. No social revolution has ever occurred in which eighty percent, or anything like it, have been generally satisfied with their lot. That is all the more true in America since the black community on the whole apparently does not wish to wreck the system, but to join it and profit from it.

One novel feature of the contemporary poverty proposals is their pessimism. In earlier days the community could be resigned to the existence of poverty as being due to God's will, and even affording opportunity for good works. In a later day, there was expectation of ridding the community of the curse by lifting the poor out of their poverty. We now assume that no remedial efforts will be effective. All commentators expect that we will truly always have the poor with us and advocate programs which will institutionalize its relief forever. That may be realistic, but we must regret the passing of the illusion of grounds for optimism. The best that is offered is the effort on the part of millenarians such as Harrington and Theobald to remove the sting of degradation from the designation of the poor. However, as long as pecking orders are found in any social group some of its members will be on the bottom. As long as the socially-useful and the socially-useless are readily identifiable, the latter will suffer low status. Victorian euphemisms will not disguise their state. The poor can raise their status only by ceasing to be burdensome.

Education offers the most likely means of lifting the able poor out of their poverty and making them socially useful. A drastic reform of education is required in order to make it fully effective, but reform is long overdue anyway. A redefinition of goals is essential for any reform. Redefining goals may also include a re-examination of the desirability of continuing all forms of education as a public service; Friedman suggests the need for another look at that particular feature of our system. As a practical matter, it appears that education as a public service is so solidly entrenched as to be unassailable. That situation has its drawbacks, as all unexamined social systems do, but at least it affords the framework for an equalization of educational opportunity. If the opportunity is to have any meaning, however, the equalization must not be in any mechanical formula such as time spent captive in a classroom or in money spent per head of pupils. Education must cultivate empirically-verifiable levels of skill in occupations by means of which the graduates can earn comfortable incomes.

The community must accept the fact that for any desired configuration of aptitudes there is a point of diminishing returns beyond which it is cheaper to support the person than to continue attempts to educate him. As cybernation advances there is a possibility that the point of diminishing returns will be reached at increasingly higher points on the ability curve, condemning ever-greater segments of the community to the role of socially-useless consumers. There is considerable uncertainty as to the effects of cybernation, however. The growth of service occupations already is marked, and they afford much opportunity for making use of persons of limited abilities. It is much too early to tell how those factors will work out in practice.

Advancing technology raises the possibility of achieving material plenty for all. Doubts as to that possibility arise from the fact that Sir Thomas More believed in the attainment of Utopia more than four hundred years ago. We are now in an affluent society, already enjoying material plenty and probably living in our Golden Age, and there are many other affluent societies. Affluence is so much a subjective mental state that the advent of the computer is irrelevant to its attainment. Cybernation will certainly increase the supply of material goods even further. Whether it will eliminate subjective poverty is much more doubtful.

We have spoken repeatedly of "socially useless" persons. Humanitarians complain that such a concept is inhumane. To charge a person with being socially useless is one of the gravest accusations that can be made; the charge implies contempt almost beneath that reserved for the criminal. Furthermore, social utility is defined differently in different communities; the utilitarian roles could easily be reversed under other circumstances. Nevertheless *this* is the society we live in, and while another definition of the socially useful could be made, there are no societies that do not have their misfits. Persons of differing personality structures might carry the onus of inutility, but someone always carries it. To be labeled as such makes a great deal of difference to the individual, but none whatever to the community; it will continue to honor whichever persons are of use to it however they may be defined. Society as a whole has everything to gain and nothing to lose by identifying those who do not measure up and affording them an opportunity for status improvement. No one in heaven or earth can compel one to use the opportunity.

We must note that one of the categories of poor relief, that of self-help in its various forms, is conspicuously missing in current proposals. We are forced to conclude that in an affluent society the persons who have the capability and skills to manage self-help systems also have the ability to become affluent, and so do not need the older cooperative devices. If the *forms* of the old self-help devices are imposed on the poor by the government or well-intentioned humanitarians, the results are meager. In fact, if they are imposed from without, as by the War on Poverty, it would appear logically that the dependency of the poor would merely be transferred to new superiors. It is difficult to see much gain therein.

A decisive check will be imposed on any welfare system adopted by a democratic society in that the consent of those just above the poverty line will limit the amount of support given. Therefore in a democratic system the degree of support afforded will be determined by striking a dynamic balance between the demand of the poor and the consent of the modestly-well-off.

Our capsule conclusion therefore is that the GAI affords the best "solution" to the problem of biological poverty. It will be supplied to a level as minimal as the poor will accept and as generous as the citizenry will afford. That level will eliminate physical need as soon as it is adopted; but the problem of subjective poverty will at best be only temporarily alleviated, to re-emerge again periodically as the economy advances. That state of affairs will continue unless there is a radical change in the social system. There is no sign of community consent to radical change, and no likelihood of successful compulsion.

BIBLIOGRAPHICAL ESSAY

The literature on poverty is so large that no attempt is made to list all of the major works on the subject. Included are only surveys through which the general reader can broaden his knowledge of areas of his interest, and which the student can use as a point of entry to more detailed special studies. Most of the surveys chosen are readily available in small college libraries and fairly large public ones. One or two uncommon works have been included when no others are available. The text and footnotes contain some additional references pertaining to narrow topics.

General

The problems of poverty are intelligible only when considered within the framework of the time and society in which they arise. Useful for providing such terms of reference are the standard surveys such as the Cambridge ancient, medieval, and modern histories, and the Cambridge economic histories.

A number of the books listed below contain a chapter surveying some of the historical methods for dealing with poverty. The most nearly comprehensive brief survey available heretofore was Sir Charles Loch's *Charity and Social Life: A Short Study of Religious and Social Thought in Relation to Charitable Methods and Institutions* (London: Macmillan, 1910). It was an outgrowth of his article on "Charity" written for the *Encyclopedia Britannica,* which is still reprinted in the current editions. The first half of the expanded book is the historical survey; the second half is an argument on behalf of continued reliance on charity as the primary means of poor relief. The bias lent his work by its polemical aspect is quite evident. Samuel Mencher in *Poor Law to Poverty Program; Economic Security Policy in Britain and the United States* (Pittsburgh: University of Pittsburgh Press, 1967) gives an even more valuable treatment of the evolution of thought with regard to poverty since the period of mercantilism: more valuable because it is more exhaustive, sets the thought into the context of intellectual currents of the day, and is more dispassionate (although Mencher was a welfarist). It is time- and culture-bound, since it only concerns modern western Europe and America. Mencher's book also ends rather inconclusively, presumably because of the author's premature death.

The problem of poverty is an aspect of the study of

economics. Indeed, if we define economics as the science of the allocation of scarcities, we might consider economics itself to be the science of poverty. Most surveys of economics deal directly or indirectly with it. The distinguished Cambridge economist A. C. Pigou wrote a full-scale treatment of *The Economics of Welfare* (London: Macmillan and Co., Ltd., 1952; first edition, 1920). The author disclaims any effort to deal with Keynes' principles (which appeared some fifteen years after the publication of the first edition); Pigou's work therefore is dated, but can still be read with profit. It cannot be easily read, however, because it is intended for specialists, and the non-specialist might easily slip into the errors of interpretation that arise from having a little learning. Non-specialists might benefit from the review and commentary on Pigou's ideas by Ben B. Seligman in *Main Currents in Modern Economics: Economic Thought Since 1870* (New York: The Free Press, 1962), but it too is pitched at a fairly austere level. Pigou should be consulted directly at least for his discussion of the meaning of "welfare." There are a number of contemporary economists only too eager to intepret economic problems for the layman; since they are hopelessly at odds with each other, they are more confusing than helpful. The principal ones are discussed in Part III.

With respect to the economics of primitive societies, Melville J. Herskovits on *Economic Anthropology: The Economic Life of Primitive Peoples* (New York: W. W. Norton Company, 1965) is a useful point of entry. The book is sparing in its use of jargon; by examining non-Western cultures the reader will be jarred loose from some of his preconceptions as to the "natural" way of conducting economic affairs; and knowing something of the methods of dealing with allocation of resources in smaller,

though not necessarily simpler, economies is an indispensable preparation for obtaining perspective on our own
problems. In a similar vein is Margaret Mead, ed., *Cooperation and Competition among Primitive Peoples* (New
York: McGraw-Hill, 1937), valuable as a selection of
essays on a wide variety of primitive societies and focused
on one of the available choices for dealing with poverty.
There are a number of excellent surveys on social/cultural
anthropology; Paul Bohannon's *Social Anthropology* (New
York: Holt, Rinehart and Winston, 1963) contains some
refreshing insights on economic problems of the primitives.

The Classical Period

H. D. F. Kitto, *The Greeks* (London and Baltimore:
Penguin Books, 1954) is a standard treatment of the
temper of the times in Periclean Athens. H. Michell, *The
Economics of Ancient Greece* (London: Cambridge Uni-
versity Press, 1940) and Tenney Frank, *An Economic
History of Rome* 2nd rev. ed. (Baltimore: Johns Hopkins
Press, 1927) afford adequate surveys of the economic
backgrounds of those states. Mikhail I. Rostovtseff's classic
studies on *The Social and Economic History of the Helen-
istic World* (Oxford: The Clarendon Press, 1941) and
The Social and Economic History of the Roman Empire
(Oxford: The Clarendon Press, 1947) are indispensable.
Guglielmo Ferrero, *The Greatness and Decline of Rome*,
5 vols. (New York: G. P. Putnam's Sons, 1907–1909)
in an appendix to volume 2 contains an essay on the
grain trade in the classical world. All of the above deal
with the liturgies; A. R. Hands' *Charities and Social Aid
in Greece and Rome* (Ithaca: Cornell University Press,
1969) will undoubtedly remain the standard treatment of

the subject for some time. All of the above also treat the subjects of slavery and debt servitude.

Medieval and Early Modern Europe

Specifically relating to the problem of church poor relief is Dr. Georg Ratzinger, *Geschichte der Kirchlichen Armenpflege*, 2nd ed. (Freiburg im Breisgau: Herder'sche Verlagshandlung, 1884), written by one who stood with one foot in the old world and one in the new; cultivated in the tradition of Christian charity, yet taking a dim view of the consequences for the poor of the growth of capitalism and foreseeing the demand for a change in the social order. Another German, Max Beer, wrote on social struggles in the ancient and medieval world and on the history of British socialism; satisfactory in its day, his work should now be considered superficial. For lack of other readily-available material, however, his *Social Struggles in the Middle Ages* (Boston: Small, Maynard and Company, 1924) can still be useful, particularly since like Loch and Ratzinger he uses a church-oriented view that is now unfamiliar. He deals at some length with millenarianism, although his book does not stand alone and is not very useful as a point of entry. E. J. Hobsbawm, *Primitive Rebels: Studies in Archaic Forms of Social Movement in the 19th and 20th Centuries* (New York: W. W. Norton & Company, 1965), has a much better treatment of millenarianism, but in recent peasant contexts and lacking a discussion of the origins of the tradition.

The Old Poor Law

England affords the best example in Europe of the operation of poor relief systems in early modern Europe.

A well-known survey is the work by Sir George Nicholls, *A History of the English Poor Law*, 3 vols. (New York: Augustus M. Kelley, 1967 [1899]). This work has a history of its own. Nicholls was not a scholar, but a ship's captain and entrepreneur who in retirement turned to public service as an administrator of the Poor Law of 1834. His liberalism and individualism were anathema to 20th-century social reformers. His work is of only slight theoretical interest, consisting principally of a compendium of Poor Law legislation useful to administrators of the New Poor Law. Since he explains and defends the principles of that law, it is now interesting also as a period piece. Nicholls was subsequently an advisor on the reform of the Irish and Scotch poor laws, on each of which he compiled similar works. Considerably more useful purely as narrative and interpretive history is Sidney and Beatrice Webb's *English Local Government: English Poor Law History: Part I. The Old Poor Law* (London: Longmans, Green and Co., Ltd., 1927). Those distinguished Fabian socialist scholars were no less biased than Nicholls, and their conclusions are considerably more attuned to the 20th-century mind, so that their work must be used with considerable care.

As to more specialized studies, W. K. Jordan presents an exhaustive statistical analysis of the operation of charities in ten selected counties between 1480 and 1660. The first and governing work is *Philanthropy in England, 1480–1660: A Study of the Changing Pattern of English Social Aspirations* (New York: Russell Sage Foundation, 1959). Additional books treat certain aspects of charity operations in still more detail. Dorothy Marshall discusses *The English Poor in the Eighteenth Century: A Study in Social and Administrative History* (London: George Routledge and Sons, Ltd., 1926). J. R. Poynter in *Society and Pauper-*

ism: English Ideas on Poor Relief, 1795–1834 (London: Routledge and Kegan Paul, 1969) makes a thorough and dispassionate study of the important period during which social forces impelled the Poor Law reform of 1834. The journalist, Brian Inglis, covers the same period in *Poverty and the Industrial Revolution* (London: Hodder and Stoughton, 1971). This is a comprehensive and readable synthesis of the descriptive literature on the conditions of the working class at that time, and also presents descriptions of the work and opinions of some obscure social reformers such as Jonas Hanway and Dr. Thomas Chalmers. He relies heavily on the books of those such as J. L. L. and Barbara Hammond who in *The Town Labourer, 1760–1832: The New Civilization* (London: Longmans, Green and Co., Ltd., 1947) and in other works present "condition of the working class" studies; they are heavily biased toward socialist reform. Most of the classics mentioned in this section have recently been reprinted.

The New Poor Law

There is an embarrassment of riches on the social history of 19th-century Britain. Certainly the best survey to put one into the picture is Élie Halévy, *A History of the English People in the Nineteenth Century*, 5 vols. (London: Ernest Benn, Ltd., 1950). General working-class social history is treated by the Fabians, G. D. H. Cole and Raymond Postgate, in *The British People, 1746–1946* (New York: Barnes & Noble, 1961) and G. D. H. Cole, *British Working Class Politics, 1832–1914* (London: Routledge & Kegan Paul, Ltd., 1941). With respect to the New Poor Law itself, it is best again to begin with Nicholls (actually Thomas Mackay), vol. III, *From 1834 to the Present Time*. The "present time" was 1899, the year in which Mackay edited Nicholls' work of 1854 and added the third volume; the occasion was the argument over Poor Law reform at the turn of the twentieth century, and Mackay's volume constituted a defense of and plea for continuation of the Poor Law of 1834. Contrasted with his views are those of the Webbs who in *English Poor Law History: Part II: The Last Hundred Years* (London: Longmans, Green and Co., Ltd., 1929, recently reprinted) present the argument for reform in the direction that was actually taken. The two are particularly interesting when read in conjunction. Maurice Bruce reflects a more dispassionate view in *The Coming of the Welfare State*, rev. ed. (New York: Schocken Books, 1966), a workmanlike monograph that emphasizes the evolution in the 19th century of the social welfare practices that ended in adoption of the welfare-state principle in Britain.

Studies on special aspects of poverty history abound. Perhaps those of broadest applicability include the Webbs on *The History of Trade Unionism* (London: Longmans, Green and Co., 1920), which is brought up to date by H. A. Clegg, Alan Fox, and A. F. Thompson, *A History of British Trade Unions Since 1889* (Oxford: The Clarendon Press, 1964). Sir Charles Loch should be referred to again, this time for his views on charity in connection with the reforms of the early 20th century. He wrote very much in the tone of the Victorian gentleman, and Loch's forty years of service to the Charity Organization Society qualified him as an expert. David Owen in *English Philanthropy, 1660–1960* (Cambridge, Mass.: The Harvard University Press, 1964) completes Jordan's work as to chronology, but "is not designed as a sequel to Jordan's monumental study." If not as monumental as Jordan's work, Owen's is nevertheless a thorough and competent treatment.

Perhaps the most thought-provoking special historical study for the contemporary social reformer would be
the relation of imperialism to social reform. In the 19th-
century context the point of entry should be J. A. Hobson,
Imperialism: A Study (Ann Arbor, Michigan: The University of Michigan Press, 1965), first published in 1902. That
was a powerful influence on Lenin and other turn-of-the-
century revolutionaries. Hobson's views should be contrasted with Joseph A. Schumpeter's in *Imperialism and
Social Classes* (New York: Meridian Books, 1960), with
separate essays on those subjects. The attractiveness of
imperialism to social reformers is evidenced by the high
proportion of imperialists among the Fabians. Since imperialism has fallen into disrepute, there is a tendency to
ignore that fact; but it has been treated adequately by
Bernard Semmell in *Imperialism and Social Reform: English Social-Imperial Thought, 1895–1914* (Cambridge,
Mass.: The Harvard University Press, 1960). Richard
Koebner and Helmut Dan Schmidt have a very interesting
discussion of *Imperialism: The Story and Significance of a
Political Word, 1840–1960* (Oxford: The Clarendon Press,
1965), which should discourage a reader from using
the word as empty invective.

Poverty in America

The suddenly-awakened interest in poverty problems
after 1963 resulted in a publication explosion, perhaps even
an overkill. Much of the spate of books and articles consisted of quickies of temporary interest. Most of those are
listed in Benjamin Schlesinger, *Poverty in Canada and the
United States: Overview and Annotated Bibliography*
(Toronto: The University of Toronto Press, 1966). It is
far from complete, being particularly deficient in histori-

206 Bibliographical Essay

cal materials; it lists only a handful of the classics. Nevertheless it is a useful point of entry for the treatment of the most immediate problems. Marcus W. Jernigan, *Laboring and Dependent Classes in Colonial America, 1607–1783: Studies of the Economic, Educational, and Social Significance of Slaves, Servants, Apprentices, and Poor Folk* (Chicago: The University of Chicago Press, 1931) illustrates the application of Elizabethan Poor Law principles in the colonial context. Robert Bremner discusses "the discovery of poverty in the United States" in the second half of the nineteenth century in *From the Depths* (New York: New York University Press, 1956). Robert W. Kelso, *The Science of Public Welfare* (New York: Henry Holt and Company, 1928), was a standard text for the training of social workers of his generation; today it is useful also as a period piece revealing attitudes of a professional social worker on the eve of the Great Depression.

A standard survey of the handling by the Roosevelt administration of the New Deal program is Arthur M. Schlesinger, Jr., *The Coming of the New Deal* (Boston: Houghton Mifflin Company, 1958). Similar in treatment is William E. Leuchtenburg, *Franklin D. Roosevelt and the New Deal, 1932–1940* (New York: Harper and Row, 1963). See also Daniel R. Fusfeld, *The Economic Thought of Franklin D. Roosevelt and the Origins of the New Deal* (New York: Columbia University Press, 1954). Most recent is Roy Lubove, *The Struggle for Social Security, 1900–1935* (Cambridge, Mass.: The Harvard University Press, 1968), a monograph by an economic egalitarian.

Helen I. Clarke not only presents a review of pertinent *Social Legislation,* 2nd ed. (New York: Appleton-Century Crofts, 1957) but sets the legislation in its historico-social context. Studies affording points of entry into special problems are William Haber and Merrill G.

Murray, *Unemployment Insurance in the American Economy: An Historical Review and Analysis* (Homewood, Illinois: Richard D. Irwin, Inc., 1966), a statistics-packed monograph; and Eugene Feingold, *Medicare: Policy and Politics, A Case Study and Policy Analysis* (San Francisco: Chandler Publishing Co., 1966).

As for poverty problems in the 1960s, it is for the most part too early to obtain much but polemical tracts. The publications most likely to be of lasting significance are discussed in detail in the text. Sar A. Levitan in *The Great Society's Poor Law: A New Approach to Poverty* (Baltimore: The Johns Hopkins Press, 1969) provides a comprehensive treatment of the enactment of the Economic Opportunity Act, together with some of the social vectors that influenced the form it took; and gives an account of the first few years of its operation. It is probably about as good a monograph on the EOA as we shall have in the near future. The author's bias toward radical extension of welfare services is quite apparent. A useful supplement thereto is Daniel P. Moynihan, *Maximum Feasible Misunderstanding: Community Action in the War on Poverty* (New York: The Free Press, 1969), which is an elaboration on the most distinctive feature of the EOA intended to dispel misunderstanding of the motivations impelling passage of that section. Ben B. Seligman, *Permanent Poverty: An American Syndrome* (Chicago: Quadrangle Books, 1968) is particularly useful for its chapter surveying the definitions of poverty. In *Regulating the Poor: The Functions of Public Welfare* (New York: Pantheon Books, 1971), Frances Fox Piven and Richard A. Cloward multiply the examples of the misery of the poor and show how the welfare system is used to support the pool of marginal laborers in times of slack employment. They also present numerous examples of special interests that manipulate the system to their own advantage. Since they begin with the Elizabethan Poor Law, historical perspective adds a very useful dimension to their study.

It is best to consult periodicals for the present status of the poverty dispute. By the end of the sixties about all had been said that there was to say and the volume of material had perceptibly tapered off. The *Congressional Digest* is useful because of its "pro and con" format, presenting transcripts of the debates in Congress on sundry aspects of poverty legislation. The usual sources should be consulted for the official views of the respective administrations. By 1968 Robert J. Lampman, a University of Michigan economist whose papers on the distribution of income were basic to much of the economic aspect of the poverty debates, was justified in publishing an article on "What We Know about Poverty," *Nation,* 207 (Dec. 9, 1968), 623–626. It would be very ill-advised to state that the last word has been said on such an engrossing subject, but Lampman pretty well summarizes the state of the debate at that time.

The Future of Poverty

The four best-known works on this subject have been treated in the text. Seligman's *Main Currents* has a very critical analysis of Friedman's views pitched at the technical level. Apparently neither Galbraith's nor Theobald's work justifies professional criticism; Harrington's is not an economic treatise at all. For an elementary treatment of contemporary economics one can with profit consult Thomas J. Hailstones, Bernard L. Martin, and George A. Wing, *Contemporary Economic Problems and Issues* (Cincinnati: South-Western Publishing Co., 1966), the principal utility of which lies in that it has been published recently enough to devote special attention to the economic problems highlighted in the contemporary discussions.

Equalization of consumption would be the logical end-product of most of the welfare programs now put forward, particularly by socialists and millenarians. On that subject consult R. H. Tawney, *Equality,* 4th ed. (New York: Barnes & Noble, 1965). This classic treatment by a distinguished Fabian economic historian is often quoted. It is intended for reading by well-informed laymen, and is therefore reasonably free of jargon.